ARRIVE:
Improving Instruction through Reflective Journaling

Additional Praise for ARRIVE: Improving Instruction through Reflective Journaling

In ARRIVE, you will discover a golden compass. Dr. Peery's words illuminate edifying and practical ways teachers and students can—and should—engage in the lost art of reflection by writing. ARRIVE *paints rich portraits of possibilities in utilizing reflective journals to examine one's thoughts and to deepen one's understanding by journaling with others. Eudora Welty said, "All serious daring starts within." If we are to grow as educators, if our students are to think deeply and achieve academic standards, we must be willing and courageous in going within to enable our children to understand the blueprints of their own thoughts. Much of our work as educators centers on helping students self-dialogue to understand and care about their learning. Dr. Peery's words radiate the true North of our work: "to enable each student to dwell in hope." We all need this text to help us navigate these essential journeys with our students, our colleagues, and ourselves.*

— Laura Benson, M.A.
International Independent Consultant and Writer
Centennial, Colorado
Adjunct Professor, University of Colorado at Denver
and Regis University
Teacher Educator and Literacy Consultant, The
National Urban Alliance for Effective Education

In ARRIVE: Improving Instruction through Reflective Journaling, *Dr. Peery articulately explores the benefits and necessity of engaging in journaling as effective, insightful, and self-propelling on-site professional development to foster the internal dialogue and reflective thinking paramount to leveraging instructional improvement and student achievement. In our constant quest for assessment in education, journaling provides compelling data for educators to mine and examine patterns of thought in order to mediate shifts in thinking and being. Dr. Peery's work unites the powerful practices of Art Costa's Cognitive Coaching, Donald Schön's Reflective*

Practitioner, and Robert Coles's narrative storytelling for learning about self.
Journaling becomes the vehicle for responding, not reacting to the
ever-changing landscape of education. Dr. Peery's examples from the field
demonstrate the power of these artifacts to connect our professional
and personal lives toward a proactive and productive experience.

— SARAH CURTIS
Educational Consultant
Designs for Thinking

I work with teachers all around the country and it is very obvious that
they are plagued by overwhelming demands that distract them from the act of
reflecting on their actions. This distraction minimizes their effectiveness
and their confidence. This book is a catalyst for motivating teachers to use
journaling as a way to maximize their effectiveness. It builds a strong
case for why journaling is such a beneficial tool including: the explanation
of the physiological benefits of journaling; the pedagogical benefits
resulting from the competence teachers develop as they use journaling to
grapple with both the content and delivery of instruction; and the
vignettes that illustrate actual, concrete successes. The explanation and
examples of the journaling process (especially **ARRIVE***) are so*
clearly articulated that teachers will feel confident in their ability to do
journaling and therefore empowered to explore the many ways
journaling can be used to optimize their teaching and learning. They
will see this book as a real tool for refining their practice and expanding
their instructional repertoire. It is an engaging guide that
will be a means for teachers to expand both their personal development
and their pedagogical competence.

—YVETTE JACKSON, ED.D.
Executive Director
National Urban Alliance
Birmingham, Alabama

In ARRIVE: Improving Instruction through Reflective Journaling, *Angela Peery makes an important contribution to the growing field of books about personal and professional balance specifically devoted to teachers. What distinguishes this book, aside from the clarity of its ideas and the power of its examples, is the time Peery has taken to back up what she says with solid research. Angela Peery tells teachers not only why they must reflect on their work and lives, but also how to do it in ways that will help them do their work better and enjoy it more.*

—JIM BURKE
Author of *The Teacher's Daybook: Time to Teach, Time to Learn, Time to Live,* and *The English Teacher's Companion*

The power of journaling is captured in a particularly enticing fabric that is woven with strategies, anecdotes, and useful approaches for teachers who are interested in addressing critical literacy skills and who also wish to integrate attention to affective issues, not only those of a cognitive paradigm. Regardless of the content subject or the grade level, this text is a must read *for all of today's teachers.*

—F. RICHARD OLENCHAK, PH.D., P.C.
Professor, Psychologist, and Director
Urban Talent Research Institute,
    University of Houston, Houston, Texas
President, National Association for Gifted
Children

ARRIVE:
Improving Instruction through Reflective Journaling

Angela B. Peery

Foreword by Douglas B. Reeves

A L P
**Advanced
Learning
Press**

Advanced Learning Press

317 Inverness Way South, Suite 150

Englewood, CO 80112

Phone (800) 844-6599 or (303) 504-9312 ■ Fax (303) 504-9417

www.AdvancedLearningPress.com

Editor: Graves Editorial Services

Design and Production: Graphic Advantage, Ltd.

ISBN-10: 0-9747343-9-X

ISBN-13: 978-0-9747343-9-2

Library of Congress Control Number: 2005928194

Printed in the United States of America

10 09 08 07 06 05   01 02 03 04 05 06 07 08 09

About the Author

Angela B. Peery, Ed.D.

Dr. Angela Peery is a teacher and educational consultant who has worked in public schools for more than 17 years, most recently as an instructional coach for English teachers at a low-performing school. She is an experienced high school English teacher, high school assistant principal, and curriculum leader at the building, district, and state levels. Along with national consulting work and writing, she currently teaches both undergraduate and graduate courses online. She is also a Professional Development Associate with the Center for Performance Assessment.

Angela holds degrees from Randolph-Macon Woman's College (1986, B.A.), Hollins College (1992, M.A.), and the University of South Carolina (2000, Ed.D.). She contributed to Teaching with Fire: Poems of the Courage to Teach *and wrote* Deep Change: Professional Development from the Inside Out.

A Virginia native, Angela now considers South Carolina her home. She lives in the coastal area known as the Lowcountry with her family, which consists of husband Tim, three Labrador retrievers, and a cat. In any spare time she can muster, she enjoys attending rock concerts, reading on the beach, boating with her husband, and spending time with loved ones.

Contents

Foreword

You are about to enter a journey of discovery. Fortunately, this journey will be about one of the most fascinating subjects you can imagine — your own personal decision-making and professional practices. As is true of most journeys, there will be anticipation, excitement, danger, and immense satisfaction.

Anticipation will precede your journey. What will I learn? Is this worthy of my time? What I can use *tomorrow*? These are fair questions by any reader for an author. Dr. Peery responds to these challenges in an inventive and provocative way. "What you will learn is your decision," the following pages seem to say. Learning is not a passive endeavor, but the result of thoughtful reflection. Anticipate challenge, not passivity.

Excitement is the next element of a journey. *ARRIVE* provides such an engaging combination of research, anecdote, and prescription that each reader who engages the text seriously will leave each chapter not only excited, but also exhausted. This is demanding, difficult stuff. Though there is no "Professor Peery" staring you in the face demanding that you do far more than you believe than you are capable of, every serious reader who takes the time to read, stop, think, and reflect, will encounter what psychologist Erich Fromm called "the most stern taskmaster": yourself.

Danger is inherent in any journey worthy of the name. When the reader engages in intellectual reflection, it is possible that the reader will be disappointed. Not a week passes in which someone does not say to me, "Surely you must have read . . ." and despite my prolific research and reading, I am clueless in the eyes of this particular challenger. The danger of publicly discussing educational research and ideas is that someone else will regard you as an illiterate, incompetent idiot if you take the risk of engaging in conversation. I have been on the receiving end of all three descriptions, and it is fair to say that I read a lot of educational research. Dr. Peery's text requires us to take these risks. Reflection—particularly in public—exposes our weaknesses. In Frank Baum's classic *The Wizard of Oz*, the memorable scene toward the end has the wizard awarding the brainless Scarecrow "the one thing you haven't got—a diploma" and the Cowardly Lion "the one thing you haven't got—a medal." Readers of this book need neither diplomas nor medals, but the stuff of which real scholarship and courage are made: the willingness to expose their ideas and reflections to the scrutiny and reflections of others. This is true vulnerability, the path to the Scarecrow's wisdom and the Lion's courage.

Satisfaction is the end of the journey, but it is an end I cannot promise. Dr. Peery offers the roadmap, but it is up to you, the reader, to follow it. There are books that I read on the treadmill, on the subway, and as I wait in line to board the 200th flight of the year. This is not one of those books. It requires careful study, reflection, and personal effort. Give it the time, intellectual energy, and personal commitment that it deserves.

DOUGLAS B. REEVES, PH.D.

Dr. Reeves is the author of more than 20 books and has twice been named to the Harvard University Distinguished Authors Series. He is the Chairman and founder of the Center for Performance Assessment, an international organization dedicated to extraordinary performance through extraordinary learning. He can be reached through the Center's Web site at www.MakingStandardsWork.com

Preface

It's true that good teachers are good for many reasons. I argue, however, that they are among the good primarily because they are more reflective than their less effective counterparts. Good teachers reflect upon their actions, continually question what they do, and strive to push their students to the very highest levels of learning. In this book, you'll meet many good teachers and will witness the thought processes they experience as they design curriculum, instruction, and assessment.

In several notable cases in this book, a teacher's increased reflection resulted in swift and significant improvement in student learning. As teachers are called upon to do more and more each day—preparing students for standardized tests, teaching to high curriculum standards, preparing students for college, creating critical thinkers, and so on—they must make time for contemplation. The examples here prove that serious thought directed toward student outcomes leads to actions that achieve the goals.

I'm grateful for being able to share the wise words of many teachers I've met through my role as their colleague, supervisor, instructional coach, and graduate instructor. I sincerely hope that you will find ideas to inspire your own work in the following pages.

Journals: A Tool for Learning and for Life

One of the biggest stressors for today's teachers is the disconnect they perceive between what they feel called *to do and what they are* told *to do. With the advent of the No Child Left Behind Act and intensified public scrutiny of schools worldwide, stress in teachers' lives shows no signs of abating.*

The unexamined life is not worth living.
—Socrates

If you are a teacher opening this book, you yourself may be torn between your desire to teach young people and the demands being placed upon you to raise various test scores. If you are an administrator charged with leading so that all children achieve at high levels, you may be looking at ways to support your teachers so that they become increasingly adept at their craft. If you are a teacher of teachers—in whatever sense, as a staff developer, graduate instructor, or educational consultant—you know very well the challenges teachers now face.

Using reflective journals should be on your list of priorities, whether you are a teacher, administrator, or teacher educator. Because humans have only 24 hours at their disposal in any given day, it is imperative that time be used wisely, with care given to continuous self-improvement. Certain reflective processes can be employed to improve one's personal and professional life; journaling is one such process.

Not only will journaling help you in your profession, but there is also evidence that it will help you in your out-of-school life as well. Forms of writing therapy have been used effectively to help people with various physical and emotional problems, including life-threatening illnesses such as cancer, chronic conditions such as asthma, drug and alcohol addictions, eating disorders, and traumatic events. Stress-related ailments, low self-esteem, and depression have all been shown to improve when reflective journaling processes are used (WholeHealthMD, 2000).

Writing has been employed to help people cope with grief. A recent example is the poetry therapists' work with the students of Columbine High School in Colorado, after the shooting there in 1999 (Whole-HealthMD, 2000). Studies have also shown that when people write about emotionally difficult events for just 20 minutes a day for several consecutive days, immune system function improves. In a 1998 study published in *Health Psychology,* college freshmen who wrote about their feelings and problems created better coping strategies and made fewer visits to the medical clinic than those who did not write (WholeHealthMD, 2000). A 1999 study in the *Journal of the American Medical Association* found a connection between writing therapy (used in conjunction with medical treatment) and relief from chronic illness (Smyth et al., 1999). Researchers found that asthma patients who wrote about difficult experiences, such as divorce, physical abuse, and car accidents, improved their lung function by an average of 19 percent (Smyth et al., 1999). Rheumatoid arthritis patients who wrote about these subjects improved by an average of 28 percent (Smyth et al., 1999). In contrast, a control group whose members wrote about innocuous subjects showed no improvement at all (Smyth et al., 1999).

Certainly there are teachers with whom you work who suffer from chronic illness, who are clinically depressed, and who are dealing with grief and loss. Though it is not up to you, as their colleague or supervisor, to "prescribe" a regimen of journaling for them, incorporating reflective writing in some fashion may help them with their problems while also helping to keep other folks in the building energized. At the very least, burnout—a very real organizational malady—may be staved off. Practices that prevent teacher burnout are generally those that allow teachers some control over their daily work. At the individual level, self-efficacy and the ability to maintain perspective regarding daily events have been described as "anxiety-buffers" (Greenberg, 1999). Using journaling to buffer anxiety and increase feelings of self-efficacy could, in the long run, help retain the good teachers at your site.

Journal-keeping is a way to slow down, reflect on one's actions, relieve stress, and plan for the future. *Journaling* (as I call the process throughout this book) is employed in schools, to help students of all ages learn academic material, and in various professions, to record important information. This book focuses specifically on how journaling has been used (and could be used) by educators to enhance professional practice, thereby increasing student achievement. (The tacit understanding is that better teachers get better results.) Although the book focuses on teachers of students in grades kindergarten through 12, some examples are drawn from instructional coaches, school administrators, staff developers, and professors working with preservice teachers.

Reflective journaling can help us all make better decisions and feel more confident in our work. Busy professionals make hundreds of decisions each day, but some would argue that no decisions have greater possible impact than a teacher's. Researchers Croasmun, Hampton, and Hermann (as cited in Starlings, McLean, & Moran, 2002, pp. 7–8) noted that the education profession has had particular difficulty inducting beginners into the complex decisionmaking processes of the job. Some teachers work with more than 100 adolescents a day; others are charged with teaching the youngest students the fundamentals of social interaction and language use. In my work with teachers, in both professional inservice and graduate programs over the past ten years, the number one complaint I have heard is that there is not enough time to do everything that is expected. Janet Allen, noted literacy author and consultant, recently said that time is the constraint most cited by educators with whom she works all across America (2004). High school teacher Jan Vescovi speaks to this constraint in the following reflection.

It just seems that there is so much to learn about teaching. I am constantly trying to read "stuff" and try new "things." There is never enough time . . . . When I hear that other teachers play solitaire during their planning [time] or read the newspaper because there is nothing else to do, I am speechless. . . . Then, little birdies tell me that the district is considering going to a seven period day, [and] I think to myself, great! More students to teach, more subject areas for which to prepare, and less time for planning! AAAHHH!

In the following excerpt, teacher Cathy Threatt demonstrates how pressure to prepare students for testing limits her choice of strategies:

Honestly, I feel that I do not have time to do literature circles . . . . There is no room in my curriculum to move, much less add in literature circles. I agree that they would be great: a wonderful way for students to learn, but time is a huge factor, unfortunately. Reading all these wonderful ideas and thoughts . . . makes me sad. I feel like I can't do anything fun or rewarding because I can't link every aspect of the activity to a standard. This drives me crazy and bores my poor students to death. I mean, if the truth were known, I am a little bored as well.

Feeling constantly pressed for time and constrained by prescribed curriculum are directly related to teachers' leaving the profession. Unfortunately, some teachers leave when it seems they are just beginning. A study published by the Northwest Regional Educational Laboratory illuminated the reasons early-career teachers depart from teaching; the NREL findings support earlier studies showing that the reasons include disillusionment, exhaustion, and lack of support (Brewster & Railsback, 2001, p. 6). According to the National Commission on Teaching and America's Future (1996, p. 13), no other nation requires teachers to teach more hours per week than the United States does; working conditions during those hours spent on the job are surely related.

Cathy Threatt's words demonstrate how teachers sometimes see themselves as mere technicians assigned to implement programs designed by others (Nieto, Gordon, & Yearwood, 2002). This frustration with lack of ownership and limitations on creativity may have increased concurrently with demands to raise standardized test scores. Journals offer a way to personalize one's experience and plan innovative ways to meet and go beyond mandates. Thomas Farrell noted that teachers feel a "sense of helplessness about their situations" (2004, p. 5). Journaling can be a way to help teachers take greater control of their thoughts and actions and can lead to dramatic improvement in student achievement, as examples offered in this book illustrate. Sheila Ruhland, in a report on teacher turnover and retention, summed up the most commonly reported reasons teachers leave teaching: career dissatisfaction, inadequate compensation, job challenges, limited recognition from administration, limited classroom resources, and student discipline problems (n.d., p. 2); in her own study of Minnesota teachers, the number one reason cited was job-related stress (p. 6). Reflective journaling and its accompanying conversations can mitigate stress and improve effectiveness.

Being an effective teacher in today's world has huge implications. Kati Haycock (1999) reported that, in a study in Tennessee schools, the least effective teachers produce gains averaging about 14 percentile points among low-achieving students; in contrast, the most effective teachers post gains that average 53 percentile points for underachievers. The Tennessee data show dramatic differences for middle- and high-achieving groups as well; it is dangerous to assume that high-achieving students can soar higher even with ineffective instruction. High-achieving students gain an average of only 2 percentile points when taught by "least effective" teachers, but an average of 25 points when taught by "most effective" teachers (Haycock, 1999). Middle achievers gain 10 points with the "least effective" teachers, but in the mid-30s with the "most effective." This data set speaks to the real issue: Students at all expected levels of achievement desperately need the best teachers the system can acquire—or the ones who can be nurtured toward high effectiveness as they remain in the profession.

Tennessee is not the only state with hard data proving that better teachers get better results. Haycock (1999) also reported the average reading scores of some Dallas fourth-graders who were assigned to three highly effective teachers in a row: they rose from the 59th percentile in fourth grade to the 76th percentile by the end of sixth grade. Another group of students that was assigned consecutively to three ineffective teachers fell from the 60th percentile to the 42nd percentile. A gap of this enormity—more than 35 percentage points—for students who started off in similar places should alarm all educators.

Similar results are evident in schools and districts that have been recognized by the U.S. Department of Education's Model Professional Development Award winners (Richardson, 1999). The winners emphasize that effective professional development must be ongoing, on-site, and focused on content that students must learn. I would add that effective professional development must focus on teachers as intermediaries or translators of content; as such, they must develop expertise in specific, high-yield instructional strategies. Skillful leaders must isolate the strategies that effective teachers use, refine them, teach them to as many teachers as possible, and employ them widely. In this manner, achievement rises. Reflective writing is important in this kind of professional development process, as it allows teachers to grapple with both content (curriculum) and delivery (instruction). This double effect makes reflective writing perhaps the most critical part of ongoing, on-site staff development.

In summary, reflective journaling is a way to lessen the stress of handling competing demands and increasing pressure. It is a way to think about past practice and make plans for the future; it helps one clarify the priorities and look at results in a nonevaluative way. It also directly affects student achievement, because a reflective teacher is a better teacher.

Jacqueline Grennon Brooks said, "Living means perpetually searching for meaning. Schools need to be places to keep this search alive" (2004). The ongoing search for deeper understanding must continue, even in the wake of current demands that seem overwhelming at times.

Journals Defined

Definitions of *journal* abound, and the word has a long history. It dates back to the fifteenth century and has its roots in the Latin *diurnalis,* which comes from *diurnus,* meaning "of the day." This definition is offered by Merriam-Webster (2001): "a record of experiences, ideas, or reflections kept regularly for private use." The Web-based BrainyDictionary.com has the following definitions, among others: "1. A diary; an account of daily transactions and events. 2. A daily register of the ship's course and distance, the winds, weather, incidents of the voyage, etc. 3. That which has occurred in a day; a day's work or travel; a day's journey."

It is interesting to note that two concepts, which may seem somewhat opposed, are mentioned most frequently in definitions of the word *journal.* One is that a journal is a record—a cataloguing, if you will—of what has happened in a day. Certainly ships' logs fit this description. Ledgers of business transactions do as well, as do the diaries of many an adolescent. The other notion is that a journal contains something deeper and more intangible than a disconnected list of events: that it contains evidence of reflection in action, on action, and for action, to borrow from the work of Donald Schön (1983).

Viewed in this light, the journal then becomes a creative, dynamic, written, verbal and/or visual artifact. In the words of E. M. Forster, "In the creative state, a man is taken out of himself. He lets it down as if it were a bucket into his subconscious and draws up something which is normally beyond his reach. He mixes this thing with his normal experience, and out of the mixture, he makes a work of art" (in Campbell, p. 129). A reflective teacher's journal can become a work of personal art that documents the time, people, and activities of a classroom and a school.

Elliot Eisner said,

> *Thoughtful educators are not simply interested in achieving known effects; they are interested as much in surprise, in discovery, in the imaginative side of life and its development as in hitting predefined targets achieved through*

7

routine procedures. In some sense our aim ought to be to convert the school from an academic institution into an intellectual one (2004).

This sounds, to me, like the personal art a teacher creates. Using a reflective journal can be an integral part of that artistry.

Journals in Various Fields

Journals in some form are used in many modern disciplines: scientists have fieldbooks, counselors maintain notes on clients, medical doctors transcribe patient files, pilots note flight data, and even scuba divers record information about each dive in a detailed log book. In all these instances, the record serves as a way to document facts, reflect on them, and prepare for future (and possibly similar) cases. Where is a parallel artifact found in education?

In education, much lip service is paid to "reflective teaching" and being a "reflective practitioner," but little time is allotted for or spent on reflection. Perhaps it is part of twenty-first-century culture, in which many people work 70-hour weeks, rush from activity to activity, and, in any "down" time, are plugged into the television and Internet, being bombarded with auditory and visual stimulation. Taking time to think, talk, draw, and write about one's experience is not a priority.

However, humans have a need to slow down and think. Short-term memory is generally believed to be from five to 20 seconds, and working memory is generally believed to consist of approximately seven units of information held in one's brain at one time. If we are to retain information, we must grapple with it in order to move it into long-term memory; Eric Jensen says "we must process it actively—for example, through discussion, art, mapping, thinking or debates" (1998, p. 105). Reflective journals can combine all the methods Jensen notes, and therefore should be employed by educators to "cement" their learning about their craft. In my 18 years of experience as an educator, I have found that we rarely make the time to think and write at length about our practice. If I did not employ reflective methods as part of every course I teach and every coaching situation in which I find myself, then even I would have very few opportunities to actively reflect, in writing or in any other ways.

It is imperative that journaling be explored more deeply in education so that teachers can perfect their craft and students reap the benefits. As Farrell aptly noted, "If teachers can become more aware of what happens in their classrooms and can monitor accurately both their own behavior and that of their students, they can function more effectively" (2004, p. 8). Educational leaders need to participate in reflective activities as well. Douglas Reeves (2002, p. 133) recommended a leadership journal focused on these essential questions:

- What did you learn today?

- Who did you nurture today?

- What difficult issue did you confront today?

- What is your most important challenge right now?

- What did you do today to make progress on your most important challenge?

If teachers continuously reflect on their work with students, and supervisors continuously reflect on their work with teachers in a similar manner, the spiral should result in a true "learning organization" (Senge, 1994).

Andrea Campbell (1993), in her book *Your Corner of the Universe,* made perhaps the best argument for personal journaling:

> *Like ingredients folded into a cake, our days blend together in such a way that we cannot distinguish one day from another, we cannot separate the egg from the oil. If we try to remember what has gone by for us, entire months are relegated to a single day's recollection, a significant or special event. Keeping a journal is one important way to counter this phenomenon . . . . Collecting and rereading your thoughts, you begin to see a canvas painted with bold, definite strokes of decision, . . . lines of pattern and direction, and filled-out spaces and achievements (p. 18).*

Douglas Reeves made a strong argument for professional journaling in his book *Making Standards Work: How to Implement Standards-Based Assessments in the Classroom, School, and District* (2004). When discussing how educators deal with the standards movement, he said, "The activity of writing reactions, reflections, and observations is invaluable . . . . Keeping a journal is an excellent means of conducting such an introspective evaluation" (p. 54).

Types of Journals Used in Education

You are probably already familiar with several types of journals. As a professional educator, you have surely either had to keep such journals yourself or have assigned them to students at one time or another. Note that within each category, there is sufficient room for the writing to be as structured or as flexible as one desires.

Amy Whited cited the following types of journals she has used in pre-service education courses in her book *The Reflection Journal* (2005):

1. **A reflective journal,** in which the person answers, "What happened? How do I feel about it? What did I learn?" This type of writing is an example of Schön's reflection-on-action.

2. **A speculation about effects journal,** in which the person answers, "What happened? What could happen because of this?" As its name implies, this type of journal focuses on anticipation of possible effects. This type correlates directly with Donald Schön's concept of reflection-for-action.

3. **A double-entry journal (DED),** in which the person chooses quotations from a text and responds to them. The quotation is often written in the left-hand column, and the response in the right-hand column (hence the name of this type of journal). A variation on this type is for the person to write in prose form, responding to something read and interspersing quotations throughout.

4. **A metacognitive journal,** in which a person primarily discusses his or her own thinking and learning. Teacher and consultant Evelyn Rothstein, in her book *Writing as Learning* (Rothstein & Lauber, 2000, p. 50), offered these sentence starters to guide metacognitive writing:

   I know that I know a lot about . . .
   I know that I know something about . . .
   I know many things about . . .
   I need to know more about . . .
   I know very little about . . .
   I know nothing about . . .
   I would like to know more about . . .

5. **A synthesis journal,** in which a person discusses what was done, what was learned, and how the learning can be applied in a practical setting. The application part is vital for adult learners.

I would add to these types a **freewriting journal,** in which a person simply writes, stream-of-consciousness style, for a few minutes at a time, in response to a prompt or other stimulus. I would also add the **collaborative journal,** in which different people make entries and the journal passes from one to another. A discussion between two people could occur in a collaborative journal; if the entries are shared publicly, as in an electronic forum, then the journal is collaborative in nature. The **learning log,** often used with students, is also ripe for exploration. In a learning log, the person writes about course content (and could write about the content of inservices as well) and/or specific questions posed by someone else.

Don't spend too long pondering the various types of journals. Instead, dive in and begin writing, using a journal as a tool for your own learning. You are not bound to use any particular type, nor to stay with only one type. Many journal entries blur the lines among the journal types, like this example from high school English teacher Cathy Threatt, writing in response to a professional book she was reading:

This chapter is predominantly about literature circles. I have not had great experience with literature circles, so it is hard for me to read . . . without skepticism . . . . I know that in these first few weeks . . . I have spent well over $100.00 on books for my students, and my existing library is by no means small . . . . Anyway, [the author] goes on to state how important it is to have your daily read-alouds tie in to something you are doing in the class, the curriculum. She mentions over and over how tying read-alouds to writing prompts really helps the kids acquire and utilize background knowledge . . . . A teacher should not begin literature circles with novels. Literature circles should be introduced with short stories, newspaper or magazine articles, or poetry . . . .

The following conversation between a teacher and me in an online class journal is an example of the collaborative format.

Teacher: *Interesting Quote: "We can choose to cover the curriculum or we can choose to teach students to inquire. If we choose to cover the curriculum, our students will fail" (Tovani [2000], 93).*

This is a great philosophy, but can we risk our livelihood to follow it? Apparently, she does not teach in a district that has strict curriculum guidelines in place and the stress of state-wide testing . . . . We are expected to follow Essential Reading Lists, to assemble Evidence Folders with specific writing entries, and to prepare students for . . . state-administered standardized tests . . . . Her strategies could improve test scores, but are most teachers willing to risk it? There are teachers in our district who have had letters put into their personnel files indicating that their students' tests scores were not "up to par." I know teachers personally who have been told that if their test scores do not improve, they should seek other "professional opportunities." I would love to go back to the days of "reading and writing workshops," but until the pendulum swings, I think I will only have sweet memories . . . .

Me: *OK, allow me to get on my soapbox for a minute . . . . Remember what Katie Wood Ray said to some of us a couple of years ago in her summer institute . . . : "What's the worst thing that could happen?" If you fall a bit short with your essential reading list or evidence folders, or your scores don't come up as much as someone . . . expects, the WORST first thing that can happen is a LETTER IN YOUR FILE. In the grand scheme of things, how bad is that? It may seem bad and upset you for a while, but . . . on your deathbed, you won't remember it.*

However, if you honestly do your best to teach the children—combined with your efforts to meet all the mandates, because you certainly don't want to be . . . insubordinate—I can bet you will have fond memories of teaching in your final days . . . . Do you want a job that is just a job, or do you want to feel fulfilled by it and know that you are making a positive difference?

If you object to certain requirements, speak up and offer viable alternatives . . . . This does not get you out of DOING them, mind you, but you live in a free, democratic society and you may express your opinions.

If you have a continuing contract, you have all the rights of the [state law], and if you are not insubordinate or incompetent, you cannot be fired without due process . . . . You are in control of what you do in your classroom, much of the time, plus you ALWAYS control your attitude! So there! . . . .

Conclusion

Teachers feel burdened with an overwhelming amount of students, paper-work, and demands for excellence. They also have busy lives, like other professionals, and find little time to make sense of their vocation, personal goals and responsibilities, and family situations. In as little as five minutes a day, however, they can achieve more of a balance and experience powerful synthesis. This freewrite by middle school teacher Wanda Freeman demonstrates synthesis:

I have to make sure I cover persuasive writing. I waited too long and now I am rushing. It never ceases to surprise me how far back I must go on the schema thing. I told the students we would write a letter to Mr. Bradley to try to convince him to use our ideas for a new exploratory class for the 8th graders next year. Man oh man if I have to answer one more question about how to write a letter, I will just die. I know knowledge once learned is learned forever. So does this mean that they really did not learn how to write a friendly letter from when they were first introduced to the concept in the third or fourth grade or when they wrote letters to their parents about their progress during first semester, or when they wrote letters to me about who they are at the beginning of school?

I have got to figure out how to get them to learn rather than memorize for the moment . . . . I have got to learn how to teach rather than cover.

In summary, why should teachers consider journaling for themselves?

- To think through and reflect upon decisions made.
- To feel empowered.
- To avoid burnout by dealing with job stress in a productive and positive way that gets results.
- To plan for greater effectiveness.

Why should an administrator consider exploring journaling as a form of staff development? Think of those folks who always speak up (and even derail) faculty meetings. Would having them write before speaking better facilitate discussion? Would more introverted teachers benefit from writing and then perhaps redrafting their ideas in memo form later? An instructional leader might consider this method to acquire more varied perspectives on the topic at hand; personally, a leader should ponder decisions made, changes proposed, results documented, and relationships created.

Andrea Campbell said, "Reflection . . . is taking the time to examine your life: to distinguish the essential from the merely important, to gain perspective on things that have happened, to identify needs, point out weaknesses, remind you of promises not yet fulfilled" (1993, p. 78). No one would disagree that reflecting on issues of importance is important in one's personal life. Shouldn't we make time to do the same for our teaching lives?

Depth over Breadth: Journals as a Key to Better Professional Development

When I reported for my first day of work in a small, rural school district, in 1986, I was eager to meet my colleagues and get ready for the students I would soon teach. On that day, all the district's teachers attended an inservice. I didn't even know what the word inservice *meant, as technically I was still "preservice." I had no idea what my first day as a professional educator would be like, but it ended with the sour taste of disappointment in my mouth.*

I love those who can smile in trouble, who can gather strength from distress, and grow brave by reflection.
—Leonardo da Vinci

My trepidation began as I entered the building, chatting with some of my fellow teachers. They were cynical: "What's it gonna be *this* year, I wonder?" and "I wish we could just go to our rooms. I've gotta get ready! I can't believe we're *here* all day. This is crazy!"

Assertive discipline was the topic. We listened to the consultant, read materials, watched videos, role-played, and wrote a basic set of school rules. As a neophyte, I absorbed a few good tips. Still, what I remember most about that day is the negative attitudes of my colleagues. Even my roommate, a usually enthusiastic art teacher who had only three years of teaching under her belt, was nonplussed. She sat beside me, silently writing her lesson plans and ordering supplies for most of the day.

My initial inservice was well intended but not well received, and in hindsight, did not result in lasting changes in practice. Therefore, it was not effective and was basically money wasted. I diligently enacted what I had learned, but within a few months, our school's discipline plan had developed into something quite different from what had been agreed to and modeled that day.

This inservice typifies many others that thousands of educators have experienced in the past 20 years. It did not result in lasting change, for several reasons:

- It was not personalized either to the learners' needs or to the local context.

- There was almost no real dialogue or collaboration; instead, the presenters relied on prepackaged materials and activities with little direct application.

- Lastly, there was no follow-up during implementation. It was assumed that the innovation would take hold and be monitored by the leaders on site, but they were ill-equipped to see the innovation through. The lack of sustained follow-up was what allowed the school, as a whole, to return to a version of its previous discipline system (which included demerits and corporal punishment) and to reinstate wildly inconsistent consequences.

My anecdote is a clear illustration of Michael Fullan's view that mandated inservices have historically not provided much beyond the technical skills teachers need (1991). Ann Lieberman has noted that teachers need a certain amount of "outside" knowledge (2000), and this particular inservice provided that. However, it did little to affect the deeper core of teaching and learning, as teachers and administrators reverted to their previous and more comfortable (although ineffective) classroom management strategies soon after the year got under way. Dennis Sparks, Executive Director of the National Staff Development Council, noted that years ago, in his talks, he would say that he thought 95 percent of staff development wasn't much good. "The first time I said it," he reported, "I expected to be contradicted. When I got up to about the 10th or the 20th time, I thought, 'I'm not going to be challenged on this. No one is going to come up to me and tell me that I'm wrong'" (Sparks, 2004, p. 55). No one contradicted Sparks because very few educators, even today, have experienced powerful professional development—the deeper, more relevant inservice education of which reflective journaling is an important component.

Relevance is a key element of effective inservice education for adults. Adult learning theory (*andragogy*) provides a framework for effective adult learning in the professions, including teaching. Andragogy is the basis for many professional development recommendations and thus deserves explanation here. To summarize and simplify, the key principles of andragogy include the following:

1. Adults need to be involved in their own instruction, meaning that they help plan it, do it, and evaluate its effectiveness. The element of self-direction is critical.

2. Learning activities must be rooted in the experiences of the participants and should be problem-based rather than content- or theory-based. In other words, practice trumps theory.

3. Adults need to see immediate, direct application to their jobs and/or personal lives if they are to be invested in the learning.

4. Adults see themselves as the sum total of their experiences; their self-worth must be honored.

Knowles perhaps explains it best himself: Adults are ready to learn something when "they experience a need to learn it in order to cope more satisfyingly with real-life tasks or problems" (1980, 44). His theories align perfectly with the standards set forth by the National Staff Development Council, which include this statement:

> *Adult learning under most circumstances must promote deep understanding . . . and provide many opportunities for teachers . . . to practice new skills with feedback on their performance until those skills become automatic and habitual. Such deeper understanding typically requires a number of opportunities to interact with the idea or procedure through active learning processes that promote reflection such as discussion and dialogue, writing, demonstrations, practice with feedback, and group problem solving (NSDC, 2004).*

The good news is that "sit and get" sessions like my initiation into the world of teacher inservice are no longer as common as they once were. For the past decade, the call has been made for more personalized and directly relevant staff development. Why has this shift taken so long to come to the forefront? As far back as 1916, John Dewey lamented, "We can and do supply ready-made 'ideas' by the thousand; we do not usually take much pains to see that the one learning engages in significant situations where his own activities generate, support, and clinch ideas." Finally, it seems, educators are understanding Dewey's ideas not only in terms of their students but also in terms of themselves. The direct link to student achievement is critical because, as many veteran teachers know, staff development was once more focused on time-saving techniques, teacher comfort, or teacher enjoyment than on student results. The NSDC claims that "teachers must experience appropriate staff development designs to facilitate the desired outcome for students" (2004).

Reflective conversation—mostly internal dialogue between the practitioner and the problem at hand—rather than the application of previously determined, readily accepted techniques, helps any practitioner learn (Schön, 1983). This is the essence of why journaling is so effective: engaging in reflective conversation with oneself allows one to create new solutions, without penalty. It allows one to criticize without retribution, experiment without failure, and celebrate without guilt.

Another standard proposed by the NSDC calls for staff development that improves student learning, deepens teachers' content knowledge, provides teachers with research-based instructional strategies, and prepares teachers to use various forms of classroom assessment. To meet this standard, the NSDC asserts that "teachers [must] participate in sustained, intellectually rigorous professional learning regarding the subjects they teach, the strategies they use, . . . findings of cognitive scientists, . . . and the means by which they assess student progress." The NSDC also calls for instructional methods used in staff development to be congruent with those teachers must use. This makes perfect sense. We educators are supposed to teach reading, writing, scientific inquiry, and problem solving, but are we ourselves being readers, writers, inquirers, and problem solvers? Are we making these processes explicit for our students? Wanda Freeman speaks to this issue eloquently in this excerpt from her teaching journal:

I know the district offers staff development on differentiated instruction, but the district fails to understand that teachers, like students, have different learning styles, different aptitudes, strengths and weaknesses. They forget that teachers are humans who must be afforded the opportunity to learn in an environment absent of fear before they can teach the children.

ARRIVE: The Reflective Teaching Cycle

An Introduction to ARRIVE

Burke and Short (1991) identified an authoring cycle that I have used with both students and teachers in many settings. The model includes bringing life experiences to one's writing; having uninterrupted personal engagements with reading/writing, collaborating, reflecting, revising, and presenting; examining one's own learning; and then getting involved in other personal engagements, perhaps out of increased interest related to the research, collaboration, writing, or reading that has just occurred. The cycle then begins anew, or may even cross over itself throughout the process.

Even though Burke and Short's model has been part of my instructional consciousness for a very long time, I did not apply it in another context until about a year ago, when I realized that it parallels a reflective teaching cycle I have observed in teachers for the past few years. I have seen the cycle in schools in which I was employed, in graduate courses I taught, and in places where I provided consulting services. Evidence from use of the cycle in various settings speaks to this truth: *Reflective teachers are constantly writing the text of teaching.* They plan, act, reflect, and then begin again. In essence, a single lesson or day of teaching is like a written draft. Sometimes, if you are a secondary teacher as I was, you get a chance to revise your drafts throughout the day. My first class was usually not the best I taught that day; perhaps it was my "fresh take" on the material, or the groggy students, or a combination of these factors. Whatever the reason, I was grateful to have the chance to compose, revise, edit, and republish as the day progressed.

The acronym I chose for the cycle is a word that gets at the heart of what we are about as teachers. That word is *ARRIVE*. We are perpetually arriving: we arrive at school each day, ready to take on new challenges. We choose goals for our instruction, and hope to arrive at those goals. We hope that our students will arrive at mastery. We also hope that by the time we arrive at the end of our teaching careers, we will have made an appreciable difference in the lives of hundreds of young people.

Here is an introduction to the ARRIVE cycle.

A = ASSESS   The teacher identifies a need or a problem in his or her instruction and/or the students' learning through some kind of measure. This measure could be a standardized test, observations in the classroom, classroom assessments, or even a school focus on an instructional issue, such as inferential thinking or essay writing. The teacher may identify the need through one or several measures. Whatever you do, though, you need real data, not just a "feeling" that the students need something or have a particular learning problem. Stage one is the *assessment* stage, in which you are assessing not only the students' learning, but your own teaching as well. You must assess the need realistically and set an achievement goal.

R = RESEARCH   The teacher researches the problem. This need not be traditional or formal research, but may consist of talking to colleagues, doing professional reading, observing other teachers, taking graduate courses, attending professional conferences, or any combination of these and other growth activities. Different teachers have different research styles, just as writers have various ways of thinking about and studying a topic before they write. Teachers should have a menu of research methods from which to choose, and then they can determine how they learn best about the particular student need being considered. This is the first "R" in the ARRIVE acronym, standing for *research*.

R = REFLECT   At this point, the teacher has been exposed to the ideas of other professionals and has probably expanded his or her knowledge base about the problem under consideration.

VIGNETTE

About 10 years ago, I became very interested in why my ninth-grade male students (mostly African-American) were so resistant to reading. I devoured several professional books about reluctant readers, informally interviewed some students, and sought help from trusted colleagues.

After immersing myself in the study of this problem for about a month, I better understood the lack of engagement. Having had all female teachers for a number of years influenced it; in interviews, the students often cited the fact that the reading material chosen for English classes did not appeal to them. Through professional reading, I found out about young adult books that would appeal to boys, so I got them. Observing my husband and two male friends discussing a recent bestseller they had all read also helped give me ideas.

With students, feeling incompetent as readers was another factor, according to both my students and the people published in this area. Therefore, I built in activities at which I knew they could experience success. Also, because they generally liked to write less and did not write as well as many of my female students, I generated other activities for them through which they could demonstrate their understanding of literature. How did I get the ideas for the new forms of assessment? Mostly by collaborating with a special education inclusion teacher, who had insight into the difficulties these students were having, whether they had IEPs or not.

My story illustrates the second "R" in the acronym ARRIVE; it's the *reflect* stage. Even though the entire ARRIVE cycle is reflective in nature, at this juncture the element of reflection is perhaps most important. Teachers must evaluate everything new they have been exposed to, either align or cast aside information that is dissonant with their personal beliefs, and determine what they are ready to tackle in their classrooms.

I = INNOVATE The teacher now identifies how he or she will change instruction, based on the preceding research and the teacher's own feelings of competence and comfort.

VIGNETTE

I am always looking for strategies to enliven reading in my classes and enjoy hearing how colleagues use drama, art, writing, and other modes of expression to engage students who were previously turned off to reading. However, I am rather uncomfortable with drama strategies. Several years ago, I experienced the use of tableaux to respond to literature. The experience was part of a workshop on strategies for teaching literature. We read an excerpt from *Snow Falling on Cedars,* and then four of us were assigned to create a tableau to symbolize our portion. We left the room, conferred, reentered, and struck our poses, staying there "frozen" while participants offered their ideas and discussed the visual image we had created and its relation to the text.

I felt awkward. First, standing still in front of a class, frozen into one position, is alien to me. I'm a real circulator in class! Second, I had to be silent. That's a difficult task for most teachers, but for me, it's incredibly hard, especially because everyone else was talking about our work of art. I wanted to prod the audience with questions.

As you may have guessed, I did not use tableaux with my tenth-grade students that year—not because it's not a good strategy, but because it's just not "me." I did, however, use some of the other drama activities presented that day, and they were very successful in reaching even my hardest hard-to-reach students.

This stage is similar to the stage Katie Wood Ray (n.d.) refers to when she asks students about their writing: "What do you want to make?" (A student could say, "I want to make a poem" or "I want to write a funny essay like Dave Barry does in the Sunday paper.") In this stage, the teachers decide what they want to "make." Do they want to make a workshop classroom? Or do they want to make a more successful research paper unit this year? Do they want to make better lessons on teaching Shakespearean drama, the solar system, or photosynthesis? The "making" can be something tightly defined in terms of time, curriculum, instruction, or assessment, or it can be something more general and overarching, such as providing greater student choice, creating a more student-friendly classroom, or providing more writing opportunities.

This is the *innovation* stage. Notice that it is not called the instruction stage. If a teacher has identified a need and conducted research, but does not implement new instructional ideas, *the cycle has screeched to a halt.* It is possible to teach the same content the same way again with no change; many educators can share examples of teachers who pull the same yellowing sheets out of the file cabinet year after year. However, if the teacher has fully embraced the earlier stages in ARRIVE, innovation occurs. Exposure to new ideas seems to refresh teachers, and once they are reenergized, they seem not to be able to go back to the "same ol' " methods. "Same ol'" just doesn't pack the punch it once did when a person has all sorts of options from which to choose.

V = VERIFY You've done the innovative teaching. That is like the publication stage of the authoring cycle, because it involves putting your work out there for the intended audience. Next you must decide where you go from here. Did the innovation get the reaction you hoped for? To answer, you must *measure* to see progress toward your goal. Compare the results of this measurement with the original measure in the first step (assess). Was there improvement? This second measurement is the *verification* stage.

You should definitely see improvement in the learning you targeted. With more intense scrutiny and commitment to the goal, the odds of increased achievement should have risen. If achievement did increase, as proven by your measurement, *continue to enact the strategies and revise them as necessary.* Eventually, the strategies that work will become part of your teaching repertoire. If they get stale (meaning they stop feeling effective for you or stop getting good results from students), choose a new problem on which to focus.

If there was no appreciable improvement in student learning, first ask yourself whether you did all the necessary research and if you chose innovations wisely. If there is any doubt, go back to the research part of the cycle and find different sources of information. Colleagues can be invaluable at this stage; seek them out! Then forge ahead anew.

If you selected strategies but did not commit to them wholly, there is a good chance that your students perceived your lack of commitment. This disconnect could have had a negative impact on their learning. Either tweak the strategies to make a better fit, or select different strategies (but only after additional research). If you have not yet done an observation of a teacher who is skillful in the techniques you're interested in, or who has had high student achievement with the goal you identified, this is an opportune time to do so. Most people do extensive research through professional reading, attending inservice sessions or conferences, and talking with colleagues, but fail to observe success in action. Direct observation of excellent teaching can be the most enlightening experience you have in the ARRIVE cycle. If a process is not in place for you to do so, approach an administrator who can make it happen, and get into someone else's classroom.

E = EVALUATE   The last stage in the cycle is the *evaluation* stage. A teacher at this stage has done some very sophisticated thinking about teaching and has applied that thinking to his or her daily work. Therefore, it's time to evaluate what to keep, what to toss, and what to tackle next.

The ARRIVE reflective teaching cycle is now complete (although, undoubtedly, every teacher has also been dealing with numerous other topics and issues throughout the cycle). To paraphrase Donald Schön (1983), we don't reflect for long periods of time without action; action and thinking are complementary. However, if you have followed the ARRIVE sequence for one important need your students have, you have committed more thought and action to that need than you previously had, all the while reflecting in action and on action (Schön, 1983) you can muster simultaneously. This is quite an accomplishment. You should pat yourself on the back!

An Analysis of ARRIVE

Let's now examine each stage in the ARRIVE cycle more closely.

ASSESS   Data for the assessment stage can come from a multitude of sources. I tend to distrust standardized test data the most—not because these tests don't give us good information (many of them do), but because the data are too old to be useful for the classroom teacher. Usually the test is given in the spring of each year, and the teacher teaches the child months later, in August or September. Another drawback: Most tests do not provide the classroom teacher with item analysis or some other breakdown that makes the data instruction-friendly. Knowing that I had a student who scored in a certain range on the "conventions" part of the state writing test did little to help me. Were the biggest or most frequent problems in capitalization, punctuation, spelling, word usage, or sentence formation? If the problems were in punctuation, were they with end marks, commas, apostrophes, or other marks? Or was there a combination of errors? It was usually more informative for me to give my own writing "test"—such as a friendly letter written to me, or a writing prompt about what the student liked and disliked about English classes—than it was to use old state test scores.

It behooves you to locate a good diagnostic test. If you can't find one, make your own (or make several). As a high school English teacher, I spent the first day of many new school years setting the mood and making expectations clear. I did a read-aloud or two, let the students participate in a discussion, and usually had them write me a letter, modeled on one I wrote and presented to them. This letter was my writing pretest. I could easily identify students who had problems with sentence structure, spelling, paragraphing, developing ideas, and organization. A bonus: I got to know my students personally right up front!

On the second day, I often gave a reading pretest, pieced together from various reading workbooks. It usually consisted of several passages, including nonfiction, poetry, and a short story or novel excerpt. The questions I chose or created were aligned with the main reading skills I would focus on (and the ones our state test emphasized): main idea, details, vocabulary, inference, and literary analysis.

By the end of the first week of school, I had a good grasp of each student's strengths and weaknesses in basic reading and writing. From there I would survey them regarding their attitudes and preferred modes of learning;

I also inquired about their academic history, family life, extracurricular activities, and goals for the future.

If you want to assess for a very specific perceived need, you can give a short pretest of your own design. For example, you may be starting a unit on state history. Give a ten-item quiz on the big concepts associated with the geography, commerce, and people of your state. You'll see right away where the gaps in knowledge lie, and you will also acquire solid information about how you can adapt the curriculum for individuals who need acceleration or enrichment, as opposed to those who need their background knowledge built quickly.

RESEARCH   The research component of the ARRIVE cycle includes all of the following (and possibly other things I have yet to identify):

- Reading print materials
- Reading online materials
- Conducting interviews of students and/or colleagues
- Viewing professional development videos
- Observing your own teaching via audio- or videotape
- Having a colleague observe you, take notes, and debrief with you
- Attending on-site or off-site inservices
- Taking a course, online or live
- Observing another teacher live
- Observing another teacher on videotape
- Talking with colleagues

Wanda Freeman exemplifies the research stage in this journal entry:

I have not written in my teaching journal because I have had nothing new to say, no new fire brewing in my chest, no sparks among the students I teach, even among the ones who profess to love to read. Yet, in my heart remained the ember of the response journal. Colleagues advised me to give it up, the pay out was not worth the work and agony paid in. But, if Abraham or Martin or The

Little Train had given up, just where would I be? I picked up my copy of **Response Journals** *and searched for the wisdom and support I once found. I scoured the Internet for ideas . . . . I used books with reproducible graphic organizers that broke each part of the response down into individual parts of the whole. I forced, no, invited, my students to read together picture books and orally share their responses on tape. I invited them to respond to jokes. I assigned one response a week so as not to overwhelm them . . . . I became obsessed with finding the secret to response journaling, so much so that the other facets of my curriculum started to suffer because I had forgotten that a good response journaling curriculum can embody all that needs to be taught and learned . . . . When [the principal] stopped me in the hallway one day to share the news that we had been awarded money because we had met AYP . . . to be used for professional books and books for class libraries, I knew I would be looking for more response ammunition. I did not have to look far.*

I found salvation . . . . Les Parsons' **Response Journals Revisited** *. . . the descendent of the book I had put so much faith into years ago when I was happy . . . called my name. I got my book today. I read my book today. I sought my journal today. I rewrote my teaching life today.*

REFLECT   Reflecting upon all the information you uncovered during the research phase is critical. This is an excellent time to write in a journal or correspond via email with a colleague who can help you clarify ideas. Wanda Freeman and I corresponded by email as part of her rethinking of some activities in her language arts classes:

I have been thinking about setting up stations or centers in my classroom, but was bogged down as to exactly how to get started. I have one reader's hand-book . . . . I have been trying to figure out how to and what to do with the MAP scores that we have. The RIT scores tell us where a student is lacking. So, if I can compile all the scores of my students and find out exactly who is lacking in which skill, I can compile folders and have students visit the files regularly . . . . I left my MAP notebook at school. I will write more tomorrow.

(continues)

This sounds like a good place for me to start in my classroom and then fan out to school. Maybe I could sell it to students who want to improve their PACT scores through the MAP results.

Take just a few minutes one day when your students are writing or working on a project and jot down the ideas you are comfortable with and/or excited by. Don't be concerned about format or syntax; just record your ideas. You may write yourself toward a solution, as Wanda did here, or you may return to your notes later and envision other solutions.

INNOVATE This is the part teachers know best: it is time to do the real work of teaching. After attending a workshop led by Ginger Manning, and after having researched her problem of lack of student engagement, Wanda Freeman tried some new strategies and shared her successes in this entry:

I had my students read, read, reread, and share with a group. The poem, "Abuelito Who," was "stupid" after their first reading. But by the time they had reread it and "talked it" in groups and waterfalled it, it came together for most of them. I asked them to try their hand at cloning the poem. As is the norm, we came up with a few good efforts.

I think I also can get good mileage with the strategy where the students rate their readings and rereadings. This gives them something to think about even if they are just trying to make the words come across their lips more smoothly. Upon trying to become smoother readers, they may work on their understanding . . . .

This could be considered differentiated instruction, as they would work at their own rate to better their skills. . . . Not until students personally assess what they know and are able to do will they intentionally buy into the idea of doing what it takes to get better. When they know where they are and we, teachers, know where they are, we can start the trip to reading success together.

VERIFY The measuring or "dipsticking" part of the cycle is imperative for several reasons:

- Teachers who implement new ideas must see that the ideas make a difference if they are to keep using those ideas; otherwise, innovation dies and the ineffective methods survive. People often return to what makes them comfortable, even if it's not getting stellar results. When I began teaching 18 years ago, I slid into the methods of my own teachers, even though I had learned many other ways to teach the same content.

- Periodic measurements provide data to outside forces (including supervisors, parents, and any other interested parties), to show how innovation is working and achieving greater student success. Why wait until a state or national test (which is designed by people far removed from your classroom) is given in April to see how you and your students fared? Instead, measure specific skills and build a more complete picture of student achievement.

- "Dipsticking" makes what is often intangible more hands-on and graspable for those who need something to take hold of (perhaps your principal). Show that you are a competent, aware professional, and "check the oil" of learning frequently. Share your results. Remember to educate students about these results, too. They need to know their own strengths and weaknesses and need to be coached into setting appropriate achievement goals.

Teachers with whom I have worked over the years experience a shift in their beliefs after student learning improves; I have witnessed this phenomenon many times. One such example was this response by Jan Vescovi, a teacher in a course for completion of her master's degree:

Now, where do I go from here? I have tried a few of the ideas from this book and feel good about those (Tic-Tac-Toe Boards, activities with SSR, etc.). I've also tried a few of my own ideas: take-out tests and focus lesson differentiation . . . . There are so many things that I want to try but have not had adequate

(continues)

time to plan. I feel like a child learning how to walk, only able to take a few steps at a time. And, I am the type of person who wants to get up and run! . . . Maybe now that testing is over (today), I will be able to actually think about those things. If not, there's always the summer.

Think about the adage, "Attitude is everything." Nowadays, many teachers express that they feel powerless and distrusted; they doubt their own efficacy, in part because others seem to doubt it. This is why the measuring part of ARRIVE is important. A teacher's shift of attitude and pedagogy most likely occurs after student learning is improved, and improved student learning is armor against unfair or uninformed criticism.

Our modern society is data-driven and information-saturated. However, not nearly enough data collection is occurring in classrooms. You need to gather data about your own teaching to show that your teaching works, especially when standardized tests are held in higher regard in many settings than teacher judgment. We must remember that these scores *never* tell the whole story. You are a better storyteller of your own teaching, so don't let number-based scores tell it in the absence of other, richer detail.

The measurement phase could possibly include any of the following:

- Teacher-made in-class assessment, whether performance-based or traditional
- Standardized tests (whether local, state, or national)
- Conferences or interviews with students
- Written, audiotaped, or videotaped reflections by students
- Anecdotal records by the teacher
- Class data, such as the number of books read per student, and so on
- Data from a computer-based school management system, such as the number of discipline referrals, scores on Accelerated Reader tests, grade distributions, and so on

EVALUATE   The evaluation stage is one of the most appropriate for reflective journaling. Once the innovations have been carried out and verification measurements have occurred, what next?

This is the time to ask yourself whether and how your innovation has resulted in increased student learning. If it has not, what do you do next? If the innovation was successful, how will you incorporate the effective practices you discovered? How will you share with your colleagues? How will you inform students and parents? What problem will you tackle next? How will you find out about effective strategies to address that problem? Writing in response to these questions can help you determine a sound course of action.

Stephen Brookfield (1995, p. 29) said, "Reflective practice is when practitioners engage in a continuous cycle of self-observation and self-evaluation in order to understand their own actions and the reactions they prompt both in themselves and in the learners for whom they are responsible." This is, in short, a description of reflective teaching. The ARRIVE cycle, even when implemented only partially, can help educators become more self-aware and, more importantly, more *student-aware*.

I hear teachers say, "We don't have time to teach anymore!" This statement may be related to goal overload, when the school is trying to do too much at one time and, therefore, everything suffers. If a teacher implements the ARRIVE cycle, even through just journaling, then he or she can at least focus on the one aspect of student learning need long enough to gauge improvement. Improvement may not be possible otherwise, because of competing goals and limited time, and the teacher's self-efficacy will be threatened. A teacher whose self-efficacy is threatened is at risk of leaving the profession—or, worse yet, of staying in the profession long after wanting to leave. An excerpt from Jan Vescovi's teaching journal speaks to this point:

The curriculum teachers are given to go by gets more rigid. This is done even within my own school by our department head. It seems that our "leaders" trust teachers less and less each year to do what is right for the students. I mean, HELLO, I did go to college, received a degree, received a masters, received a masters plus 30 [credit hours], and continue to take classes each year to make me a better teacher. This is the daily struggle that I face.

The reflective teaching cycle is, at its core, very creative. Because we are in a time of rather uninspiring mandates, it is liberating and empowering to be able to think and act creatively. Joseph Campbell, a scholar and writer, noted, "You can be reactive by passively adjusting to whatever life throws at you. Or you can be reactive [proactive] and work on a specific problem until you find the right path or solution" (quoted in A. Campbell, 1993, p. 42). The essence of ARRIVE is to be proactive and take matters more firmly into your own hands, knowing you have the power to enact positive change.

VIGNETTE

At one school where I worked, we were focusing on all these things one year: the state's writing rubric, writing across the curriculum, silent sustained reading, Accelerated Reader, critical thinking skills, vocabulary improvement, improving the behavior of students, increasing attendance, teacher teaming, interdisciplinary projects, hands-on activities, increasing parent involvement, using technology . . . . Tired yet? The "focus" was too dispersed. Therefore, many teachers felt that they were trying everything and succeeding at nothing.

If you are a teacher at a school with a hodgepodge of goals like I just mentioned, pick one that is directly linked to your content area and to something more in your control. For example, you may not be able to control much about the dropout rate, but you're able to control a good bit about improving students' writing skills. Even if you are a math or physical education teacher, you know what a good sentence is and what a good paragraph is. If you can get students to write about math in sentences and paragraphs, then you are helping them gain competence in writing. This work may even lead to discussions of writing style and conventions in your class. How exciting! Also, you are getting them to articulate what they understand about math. You can support the work of the main writing teacher, the English teacher down the hall or on your team. The bonus is that students begin to see that writing is important to more than just one teacher and in more than one subject. If writing is important across the board, then children will do better in writing across the board. They may even begin to perceive its importance in the world outside school.

The school with the myriad of goals did implement a very focused, school-wide approach to content and organization in writing in the spring of one school year. The results were amazing. We did our own writing and scoring in all content area classes; we taught mini-lessons on errors we saw repeatedly and on how to develop ideas and organize essays. That year's state test scores were the highest the school had ever had in writing. Coincidence? No—teamwork, reflection, and focus.

As Douglas Reeves has said in both his publications and presentations, it is important that educators "weed the garden." Some goals must be deleted as we choose and concentrate on those we deem most important.

Here's how to make a difference, even if only in your classroom. Pick a goal you are personally invested in and that matters in your subject or grade level. How can you tell if it matters? This is not just a matter of your personal opinion: consult state and national curriculum documents before selecting the need or problem you will move through the cycle with, and don't forget to cite credible measures to document that there is a deficiency you want to address. In the words of Douglas Reeves, choose those standards or learning goals that are enduring, provide leverage, and prepare students for the next level of education (quoted in Ainsworth, 2003, p. 15); or, in the words of Larry Ainsworth (2003), make sure they are important in life, in school, and on the state test (p. 16).

Asking "what if" is also important. "What if?" is extremely creative. Remember, even small changes can have *huge* impacts. One time I added silent sustained reading (SSR) just two days a week for 20 to 30 minutes each time in my ninth-grade English classes. The change in the culture of my classroom was incredible! The kids begged for more time. One of my ninth-grade honors students started a graffiti poster board of interesting quotes. Another student started a "poetry corner" and others found poetry they liked and displayed it in response. One special education student's reading level rose two grade levels in just a couple of months. This inquiry, and the improved instruction that resulted, began with asking myself, "What if I provide reading time in class? Will this help the students become better readers?"

To close this discussion of the ARRIVE teaching cycle, Mikhail Baryshnikov's words are appropriate: "I do not try to dance better than anyone else. I only try to dance better than myself" (quoted in Campbell, 1993, p. 144). As a teacher, one should not try to compete with colleagues, but instead should try to dance one's own best dance. Reflective teaching that makes use of the choreography discussed in this chapter will result in greater artistry and improved performance.

What Do We Mean When We Say **Journaling?**

Reflection is the essence of growth. In this chapter, I would like to paint the concept of reflective journaling in broad strokes and to offer powerful examples of the different types.

Writing is thinking on paper.
—William Zinsser

Briefly, the types of reflective journaling I have encountered in the past decade, as both a participant and a facilitator, are as follows:

- **Written journals** (private, collaborative, or public; either handwritten or word-processed)

- **Art journals** (including those employing graphic organizers, doodling, sketching, painting, collage, etc.)

- **Verbal journals** (meetings in which people speak in turn on a specific topic, sometimes after writing about it first)

- **Electronic journals** (email and instant message conversations, distribution lists, or bulletin boards)

Journaling may take place at any step in the ARRIVE cycle. In the first stage (assess), journaling may help a teacher make sense of a perceived problem. Data can be recorded and analyzed. In the second stage (research), notes from the teacher's inquiry can be recorded and reflected upon. Significant ideas from reading, discussions, and other forms of research could be added to the journal. Tentative plans can also be written about in rough draft form. In the third stage (reflect), the teacher must make a decision about what to do next. If journaling has been used in the previous two stages, the journal can be reviewed; this may help clarify what should be done next. The fourth stage (innovate) then occurs. During this stage, the teacher may feel so busy that she or he does not make time for journaling; however, it is crucial that, at minimum, snippets of information be entered into the journal. These snippets will become important later when the teacher decides what to keep, revise, and discard. The fifth stage (verify) is when the teacher measures student achievement based on the goal set in stage one. Results can be recorded and analyzed in the journal. In the last stage (evaluate), the teacher plans how to integrate the innovation into her or his practice, how to modify it for greater effectiveness, or how to discard it and find another innovation that offers more promise.

The ARRIVE cycle mirrors the five core propositions of accomplished teachers, as stated by the National Board for Professional Teaching Standards (NBPTS). The NBPTS proposes that teachers think systematically and learn from practice. The organization asserts that

> *accomplished teachers are inventive . . . and, recognizing the need to admit new findings and continue learning, stand ready to incorporate ideas and methods . . . that fit their aims and their students. What exemplifies excellence, then, is a reverence for the craft, a recognition of its complexities, and a commitment to lifelong professional development (n.d.a).*

Furthermore, teachers demonstrate "the ability to reason and take multiple perspectives to be creative and take risks, and to adopt an experimental and problem-solving orientation" (NBPTS, n.d.b). To become a National Board certified teacher, one must create a professional portfolio, among other assigned tasks. Journaling can be a productive process to use in conjunction with National Board certification (though it can also be tremendously helpful on its own).

Written Journals

Written journals may be very informal and unstructured, or more formal and highly structured. They may be kept totally private, voluntarily shared with a trusted colleague, shared in small groups, or made public in a number of ways. Entries may be written in response to various prompts; in response to reading, viewing a videotape, or participating in a presentation or workshop; as part of formal evaluation or a formal professional portfolio; or they may be made spontaneously, at the discretion of the writer, as he or she sees fit.

Here are some ways in which I have employed written journals with adults in my career as a public school educator:

- **As a teacher and team leader,** I used reflective writing myself to plan instruction for my students and meetings for my team.

- **As a presenter,** I asked audience members to do "quick writes" of two to five minutes at various points in a session. I have also asked them to complete "entrance slips" and "exit slips" on index cards.

- **As an administrator,** I required teachers to write self-reflections after viewing videotapes of themselves teaching.

- **As a staff development consultant,** I have started meetings with writing prompts related to the content of the session. Most of the time, all the participants and I write until everyone arrives, and then the conversation ensues.

- **As a graduate school faculty member,** I require students to keep reflective journals throughout the duration of a course. Often these are sent electronically to all members of the class; sometimes, most of the entries were written in response to professional reading and to presentations attended.

- **As the co-teacher of a National Writing Project summer institute,** I use written and art journals to get teachers to think about their teaching and to involve them in the writing process themselves.

Mary Heflin, a middle school teacher who was teaching language arts for the first time in many years after having taught math, kept a reflection journal over the period of a semester as she was enrolled in a graduate course I taught. This journal was shared with only one person (me, the instructor). Notice how she focuses on individual students (Taylor), subgroups of students (inclusion), and her own teaching. Also significant is the enthusiasm she expresses: this positive emotion is one of the best deterrents to burnout.

March 31

Poetry is wonderful! Today Taylor read his autographed copy of "Blond Chicks Rule" [a poem] for the class. He said he had to get in the mood and asked the class to be quiet. He read the poem with the appropriate facial expressions and gestures in a voice that would perfectly fit a 13-year-old girl.

April 16

. . . We discussed catastrophic events on earth—tsunamis, meteors, . . . and then connected them to the myth. In partners the students brainstormed a catastrophe, wrote, and presented a myth . . . . Their ideas were great. One was "why there are curse words," [which] strayed from the natural disaster formula but [they] understood the myth idea perfectly. I now see what can be accomplished in one block (70 minutes) even by resource inclusion students.

April 19

We reviewed main ideas and themes using the [workbook]. I like this book because it gives very good definitions. It also gives the students practice . . . responding in 2–3 sentences or paragraph form, and also practice with multiple choice. I am also able to better point out test taking strategies. I feel it might have been better for me to use these lessons spread out over the year [instead of only in the spring]. A picture and plan for next year (and hope and anticipation) are definitely coming into focus for me.

April 22

Today we reviewed the poetry unit for PACT [the state test]. From the assessment, it appears that overall the students successfully learned the vocabulary for the test. I plan to prepare a "Jeopardy" game based on the vocabulary in the literature book and the . . . curriculum standards. I will use this to review the Friday and Monday before the [English language arts] PACT.

Here is an example of journaling by teacher Wanda Freeman. This entry was shared publicly, in a presentation of a personal inquiry project Wanda carried out in her classroom. Her project was based on teaching poetry.

I could feel the immersion. I dove right in and nearly broke my neck at the bottom of the poetry pool. I had forgotten to fill the pool with poetry knowledge. I had to regroup . . . . I had to change my quest from "how can I increase certain comprehension skills through the study of poetry?" to "how can I differentiate instruction throughout a unit on poetry so that all students may experience success with . . . understanding poetry . . . as well as writing . . . their own?" Assuming too much, I had attempted to toss my students into the pool of poetry before they could swim. I had failed to first measure their swimming ability . . . . Once again in my teaching life, I would be learning new strokes as I swam along, all the while praying that they would not pull me under while I was trying to save them.

This entry clearly highlights the need for teachers to do the preassessment step (the first stage) in the ARRIVE cycle. Wanda did not give adequate attention to that step and thus had to "regroup" later.

Wanda made good use of the innovation stage, however, even using one of her own poems to assess students later in the project. This could be considered her preassessment measure, although it was given too late (see Appendix A for Wanda's materials).

Lisa Haselden, a high school teacher, completed an inquiry project on the effective teaching of vocabulary to her students. The three classes with which she used innovative methods, and tracked data by jotting in a journal, consisted of 25, 22, and 19 students, respectively. By the end of her project, she noticed that the students were even using words authentically in conversations, and 73 percent of the students improved their scores on SAT vocabulary quizzes. In the following reflection, shared publicly as part of a presentation to colleagues, Lisa celebrates success:

My students have been exposed to meaningful and engaging ways of learning . . . new vocabulary. I have learned that there is no excuse for giving students a

(continues)

list of words to look up in the dictionary and use in a sentence . . . I have learned that this inquiry does not end here and that I must continually strive to provide effective vocabulary strategies for my students.

Renea Stephens, another high school teacher, shared this written reflection with a graduate class:

So many of my students come into class thinking they are poor readers. On the first day of the class I ask them to answer this question: Are you a reader, writer, or both? . . . I believe the reason most do not consider themselves readers is because they don't like to read. They don't like to read because they are not reading things that interest them!

At the end of the semester I ask the same question. I usually see a shift in the numbers [of those saying they are readers, writers, or both]. Why? . . . 1. We read every day. 2. We write about what we read every day. 3. I encourage them to read what they like every day. 4. I encourage them to abandon a book if they do not like it . . . .

As the preceding examples illustrate, written journals, even if done only sporadically, can produce real change.

Art Journals

Sometimes capturing your thinking symbolically is more powerful than doing so in words. For some teachers, art opens up the reflective process wider than writing does; for others, however, it can seem to hinder the process, at least initially.

One of the most powerful questions I have ever invited teachers to explore —using art, or writing, or a combination of both—is: "What metaphor best captures your teaching or your classroom?" When I first did the metaphor activity as part of a group of teachers, my metaphor was that of a poet. See Appendix B for my symbolic representation. Cathy Green, an elementary school special education teacher, captured her image, that of a hummingbird, in a sketch using oil pastels (see Appendix C).

In a culminating activity for a graduate course, my co-instructor and I asked teachers to visually represent how they would take their learning back to the classroom. One teacher's response included a drawing of an ant that had climbed a mountain. The caption read, "Give me the freedom to move. Let me express the words I see with my hands, legs, arms, but don't enclose me within words alone. Let the words speak not just from my lips, but from how I perceive the words in my mind and heart and then convey to you, as I move."

Verbal Journals

Verbal journaling is not the typical talk of teachers' lounges or outings on Friday afternoons. It is purposeful, thoughtful, and structured so that each person has a turn to respond. Time may be reserved for questions and statements of appreciation or empathy after everyone has spoken.

I employed various incarnations of verbal journaling over a two-year process of consulting with the Chabad Academy in Myrtle Beach, South Carolina. To show how the process can work, here are my complete notes, word-processed after being written initially in the meeting in March 2000.

I arrived late—about 3:35 . . . .

Leah [principal] told me before we got started that she is teaching a Bat Mitzvah . . . class and is using journals. She ordered a curriculum for the class but found that she did not like it . . . . However, she already had bought the girls journal notebooks like the ones we use . . . . On the first day of the class they wrote about the topic "relationships." The girls enjoyed writing so much that they asked if they could write more. Leah also modeled writing in a journal, as she wrote while they did.

I asked Leah why she thought they wanted to write more. She said she thinks she chose a rich topic (which was suggested in the purchased curriculum); she served as a model; and as a teacher, she gave time and value to the assignment.

(continues)

Sara [teacher], Leah and I continued to talk as we waited for Vivi [teacher] . . . so we could all do our journal writing together.

Sara brought up the topic of repeated misbehavior and forgetfulness in her classes. She said she has to repeat instructions several times, even for her brightest students. She notices that they are often off-task and inattentive. She said she really wants class to run smoothly . . . . I asked her, "What strategies have you tried that don't work?" She said she repeats directions mostly when asked and reminds students continually of what to do. She even sent a letter home earlier in the year telling the parents what she expects. She said she has noticed that grades are important to students. Lately, she has learned to have them ask a classmate when they need a direction repeated. This has worked well. She said she is very frustrated that they forget their supplies. I gave her two suggestions: have supplies on hand and make sure they know it is their responsibility to get the supplies before class starts and not to interrupt class . . . . Have students without paper or pencils work their problems on the board for everyone to see. If it bothers them, they will start to remember their supplies . . . .

Vivi entered the meeting . . . . We all wrote for 5 minutes on the topic, "How did your teaching change in the past year?" Then we wrote for 5 minutes on the topic, "How would you like your teaching to change in the next year?" Then we began sharing from our entries.

Vivi . . . wrote about what she wants to change for next year and all that she feels she needs to learn. She also has concerns about discipline and feels that it is hard to be "friends" with the students . . . but also to discipline them . . . . She expressed a sense of inadequacy.

Sara said she has noticed that teachers are very hard on themselves . . . . We discussed reflection time, journal writing, and collaboration . . . . Leah said that "time for reflection is like homeopathic medicine . . . ."

Sara shared from [the journals she] has used . . . in her Hebrew classes.

Although the meeting seemed fluid and somewhat informal, the questions we wrote about and then discussed in a structured fashion got the teachers to think about their craft and set goals for improvement.

Following is an example of an agenda from a meeting with the same group of teachers. This meeting was different because it was during a year in which we had chosen to study a book together. The book was *Classroom Instruction That Works* (Marzano, Pickering, & Pollock, 2004). This meeting utilized the verbal journaling process very effectively and demonstrated how verbal journaling can be orchestrated to enhance group study of a professional text.

Chapter 5: Homework and Practice

What is the difference between homework and practice?

What is your main purpose for homework? Are there other purposes? (See p. 63)

Agree or disagree: Parent involvement in homework should be kept to a minimum.

What is one of your best homework assignments?

The conversation (verbal journaling) was at its best in this meeting when discussing parent involvement. That point became a real teaching opportunity for me to lead the participants in an honest dialogue about the purposes of homework as it relates to academic achievement. I think several of the teachers walked away having revised their ideas about assigning homework for responsibility reasons, instead of assigning it for each child to achieve at higher levels.

National Urban Alliance consultant Carlton Long begins many of the inservices he facilitates throughout the United States with this question as a verbal journaling prompt: What has to occur here today in order for this to be a worthwhile learning experience for you? As the participants respond, they are articulating their goals for the session, and Carlton is allowing them to take ownership. He also gets good information up front about how to personalize and make relevant his session.

Purposeful conversations around the issues of student achievement and teacher methods must be facilitated. Verbal journaling is one way to talk about these critical topics.

Electronic Journals

Even though electronic journaling must be written first (at least typed), I have included it as a separate category because it is a relatively new phenomenon and has risen to popularity. During the 1999–2000 academic year, as I was completing my doctoral course work, I had to post responses electronically on a class discussion board, but this was the first time I had been required to do so in more than 12 years of graduate school. Now, posting and emailing responses are almost commonplace in graduate courses. This increase illuminates the real need humans have to process new learning linguistically and to share it with others. It also highlights how technology has become a crucial means for people to work and learn collaboratively.

I have done instructional coaching by electronic means in the past two years, with teachers in my graduate courses and teachers I meet as a consultant and presenter. Here is an example of one of many coaching conversations a teacher and I have had. This teacher teaches remedial reading in a middle school and was in the beginning stages of an inquiry project.

Teacher: *Question: How can students learn reading comprehension strategies and make them their own?*

Goal: Help students develop a love for books.

Me: *I would narrow the actual question down to 2–3 strategies new to them, since you have a short time for the study, and it's easier to measure your progress if you really focus.*

Teacher: *Pretest Measures: 1. A survey on what makes a good reader and asks the students to list their favorite genres. It will also determine the students' self esteem as a reader.*

Me: *I would have them check things off a list (strategies) that they use; for example: rereading, using a dictionary, asking a friend to help, reading the passage out loud, etc. (Tovani's book can help you.)*

Teacher: *2. PACT scores from 2003*

3. MAP Reading scores from Fall 2003 and Winter 2003

4. Reading Response Journal entries

Me: *2–4 are all fine as is. You can measure "love of books" in the response journal entries.*

Teacher: *Classroom Methods: 1. Daily mini lesson of Tovani's six strategies, "How do I know when I'm stuck?" (page 38.)*

Me: *Great—model all and then have students evaluate the 3 they use most often at the end of the unit—the 3 they think they will continue using . . . .*

Teacher: *2. The teacher will model one reading comprehension strategy each day of the week, one strategy per week. These will be used more as reading comprehension strategies, rather than fix-up strategies.*

3. The students will choose and read high interest novels by themselves or with partners. The students will be asked to practice one strategy as they read.

Me: *One strategy per week? More than one strategy for a book, right?*

Teacher: *4. The teacher will conduct conferences with the individual students focusing on Tovani's six reading comprehension strategies. This will allow for individualized instruction and give the student the opportunity to demonstrate the reading comprehension strategies orally and higher level thinking.*

Me: *I want to see you keep a Nancie Atwell-type chart or something to document each conference. It can be a quick notetaking system; I may even have a template you can use. This will be DYNAMITE to document individual progress.*

Teacher: *5. The students will complete reading responses in their journals. Responses will provide the students with the opportunity to demonstrate reading comprehension strategies on paper.*

Post Test Measures: 1. The students will complete the same survey they took for pretest methods to determine a change or growth in comprehension strategies and self confidence.

2. The students will be given a quiz to determine whether or not they can recognize and use these reading comprehension strategies.

Me: *OK, why the quiz? Is this taking the actual strategies a bit out of context? Isn't the true assessment whether or not they can use the strategies?*

Teacher: *3. The students will be given excerpts from textbooks to see if they can transfer skills from enjoyable novels to dry reading. This will help determine if the students have "made these strategies their own."*

Me: *GREAT!!! I'm very interested in this part! Everyone else will be, too.*

Following is an example of an instant-message conversation I had with teacher Wanda Freeman. This conversation is representative of many I have had in the past few years (but unfortunately, I didn't log most of them!). Notice the informal nature of the language. All our original misspellings, etc. have been left as is. (The teacher's screen name is Kindred216, and I'm Angela7145).

Kindred216: *I was journaling today about jsut what it is I want to figure out with my research question. I want the students to improve their reading strategies throug the study and writing of poetry. However, when we study poetry I am not really using the strategies such as main idea, inferencing, cause/effec, drawing conclusions. I feel like I am forcing the question.*

Angela7145: *the main idea of a poem is really theme*

Angela7145: *inference is all throughout poetry*

Angela7145: *so take a poem and a companion essay or nonfiction piece*

Kindred216: *We ARE GETTING LOST IN THE JOY OF POETRY and I am not sure how to make the connection I thought I saw between teh analyzing of prose using the stratigies. I am not sjure if I want to make inferences in poetry and then jump to making inferences in prose. I also think that I shall narrow the strategies down to three instead of five. Inference I can see. We did have a time with theme on friday I guess I will have to just keep at it. I was thinking about Bronx Masquerade. I got into talking about respondin*

Angela7145: *go for the 3 instead of the 5 for sure*

Angela7145: *the tighter the focus, the better! you can concentrate that way.*

Angela7145: *and see results.*

Kindred216: *and then turning that prose into poetry. Do you think the responses and corresponding poems are too close to lookat inferencing because once you see it in the poems, you automatically see it in the prose. Should the two pieces be closely related*

Angela7145: *well similar viewpoints or characters in similar situations . . . you decide*

Kindred216: *The other day you suggested that I may have too much assessment in my plan. So do you think the study and assessment we do will/should automatically transfer to PACT. Do you understand my question?*

Angela7145: *hmmm . . . not really. tell me again.*

Angela7145: *i think you don't need a big project and a test*

Kindred216: *okay, I said that I would pretest. Then I would test on the elements and reading strategies with teacher made assessment. Then I would test them with PACT like assessments. You suggested that three assessments might be too much, that I might offer a choice of a teacher made test or portfolio that demonstrates knowledge of elements and reading strategies. I am wondering if they would transfer thier knowledge to the PACT*

Angela7145: *Knowledge is knowledge; if you have it, you can show it on pact. you must have the deep understanding FIRST*

Angela7145: *you have to do a pretest. after instruction, offer them one post-measure: either a test with pact-like items and other items on it together *OR* a portfolio/project.*

Kindred216: *Then that is where i shall be going. Devil may care how long it takes some kids to get it. This is where differentiation comes in. but I have to really talk things out these days to see where I am going. I know that Amy in 6th block will be able to start on her portfolio in a few days while Chris will have to work with 50 poems.*

Angela7145: *yep! and that's the essence of differentiation*

Kindred216: *I am getting clearer now. Thanks for listening. I will let you go now. I am sure you did not expect ot be teaching jsut now.*

The Future of Journaling

Certainly there are forms of journaling in which I have not participated, facilitated, or even envisioned. As technology gets more sophisticated, the human need to reflect and to communicate will remain constant, but the methods will evolve. Journaling (in all the forms represented in this chapter) is a powerful tool, however, and should be fully employed in educational settings so that educators become more cognizant of their thought processes as well as their actions and the impact of those actions.

Written **Journals** in More Detail

Written journals contain evidence of a wide range of reflective thinking. After examining the journal entries of more than 100 teachers in the past eight years, I have categorized the types of entries I've seen as outlined below.

CHAPTER

Teachers who teach for meaning also make time to wonder.
—Jacqueline Grennon Brooks

4

1. The teacher is examining his or her own learning. I call this category *metacognition.*

2. The teacher is examining his or her own teaching, including issues related to learning climate, student management/discipline, curriculum, instruction, and assessment. I call this category *instruction,* as it focuses on instruction and all the tangential issues in the classroom that directly affect instruction.

3. The teacher is examining student learning by examining whole classes, subgroups, and individuals. This category I call *achievement,* to keep the focus on the students and their learning.

4. The teacher is celebrating his or her own success, the success of students, or both (as they are usually interrelated). I name this category *affirmation.*

5. The teacher is venting frustration. This category I call *dissatisfaction.*

6. The teacher is creating new solutions to problems. This category I call *invention*.

In summary, the six classifications I propose are metacognition, instruction, achievement, affirmation, dissatisfaction, and invention.

Thomas Farrell said, "By writing in a teaching journal, we freeze our work so that we can reflect deliberately on it" (2004, p. 74). The teachers whose entries I have been privy to, either as a colleague, instructor, consultant, or peer coach, have come away from the writing process more sure of their own philosophies of teaching and more willing to take risks. They have increased the amount of professional reading they do and have generally become more collaborative, by networking with peers, joining professional organizations, and attending conferences.

John Dewey was certain that when teachers combine experience with reflection, they grow professionally (1958). In a simple analogy that I use repeatedly: If you're not ripening, you're rotting. Writing in a teaching journal is one way to ripen.

It is important to note that a teaching journal is not a griping journal. *Complaining without thinking creatively to develop possible alternative actions is a waste of time.* In other words, if you decide to write in the dissatisfaction mode, you must be sure also to move yourself to the invention mode, or your reflection will be unproductive. There are plenty of mere critics of educators already out there. Those of us within the profession must relieve ourselves of our frustrations, surely, but we must also work toward improving ourselves and our craft in order to best serve students.

Journal writing can serve purposes beyond your own professional development if you choose to share what you have written. Diane Freeman said, "Teachers and learners know the story of the classroom well, but they do not usually know how to tell it, because they are not often called upon to do so, nor do they usually have opportunities" (1996, p. 101). I urge you to take the opportunity to write for yourself, and then consider turning your work into something more public, perhaps an article suitable for publication in a professional journal. (This is how my own publishing journey began.) Politicians, parents, business and community members, and pundits of various media try to tell the story of the classroom constantly, and they are not living it day-to-day as teachers are. We must be more articulate about our work and seek wider audiences.

Cathy Threatt provides an example of metacognition in this journal entry:

It is really important that teachers model making connections to literature. And, it is also important for teachers to have wrong answers and make mistakes with their students. Students expect us to automatically know the answers to all their questions and they are amazed when I say, "I don't know, but I will find out for you." Sometimes I end up learning neat stuff in the process.

In the following journal entry, high school English teacher Jay Philon exemplifies the teacher who is becoming more sure of a teaching philosophy and also shows the characteristics of invention:

On every job interview I have had . . . I have been asked if and how I teach grammar. At the time, the "if" surprised me . . . . The problem started when all those studies came out that said that teaching grammar did not improve a student's ability to write or keep a student from making the very errors he was being taught to avoid. At that point, educators threw the baby out with the bath water . . . . Now, I am faced with 10th, 11th and 12th graders who do not know a noun from a verb, and I mean that literally.

. . . Knowing basic grammar—the names of the parts, and the basic do's and don'ts of your own language—is just plain core knowledge . . . . It gives us a common terminology . . . . Granted, not everyone will get real good at it, but not everyone takes calculus either . . . . That doesn't mean we stop teaching adding, subtracting and multiplying, now does it? . . .

With that said, most foreign language teachers spend as much time teaching grammar as they do their target language. So, instead of a foreign language reinforcing English, foreign language has been forced to pick up the slack of a

(continues)

failed experiment. If taught correctly, grammar is a vital first step in under-standing the written language. It is foundational, but it is a means, not an end. The problem is, . . . for years, English teachers taught grammar as an end in itself. Which means once they drilled the parts, they just stopped. The practical application of the knowledge . . . just did not happen effectively. But instead of scrapping the whole system, why not modify it to face its most just and terrible criticism? . . .

Another major problem that is just beginning to surface—we now have a generation of English teachers that are very weak in grammar, if they have had it at all. In a 400-level grammar course [for teachers] I recently took, well over 75% of the class had never had grammar taught to them . . . .

The fault lies not in the drill and kill system of isolation, but the fact that the knowledge gained there was not practically applied in student writing. A student was taught grammar, then wrote a research paper about literature. There was little done to connect the two . . . . Along that line, I believe sentence combining and having students create sentences using the parts of speech prac-tically applied hold some of the answers to the grammar puzzle.

. . . If the whole focus of learning grammar is to use it to improve your writing, it will; and, at the same time, grammar will give the student the foun-dational knowledge needed to springboard into other disciplines . . . . Unfor-tunately, there are few textbooks that even address the issue of grammar in any detail, much less present a progressive use of grammar in writing situations.

I have been working up a system of my own, but . . . other aspects of cur-riculum have slowed the process. Ultimately, I will design a system that begins in isolation, but quickly pushes the student to create sentences and paragraphs using the grammar concepts just learned. Ideally that system will seamlessly integrate with the other aspects of the curriculum I am teaching . . . .

Jay epitomizes the reflective teacher as he makes his concerns known but also explains what he is personally doing to address them. He exemplifies a "ripening" teacher! He has found a learning need he must address in his classes and has also found a gap in the learning of other English teachers. This entry is ripe for revision into an essay for an English teacher's publi-cation or even for the op-ed column in the local newspaper.

Teachers often examine student learning in great detail in journal entries. This is worthy reflection, as it results in changed teaching. For example, here is one entry by Cathy Threatt that shows how she is focused on specific subgroups of her classes:

I am really excited about using this [idea] with my short story unit. Yes it is going to take extra time, but I am focusing on quality not quantity. Right? And, since students will have to write on one of these short stories for their [county test] prompt, this will help really imprint the story in their heads. I have a big plan for "Everyday Use" anyway, so one or two more days isn't going to kill me. I am also hoping that this will draw out some of my low-level kids. I have a few that just cannot get what is going on in class, so maybe this three-step activity (me modeling, group work, individual work) will help them comprehend and get involved . . . . I also liked the fact that [the presenter] typed out the children's book . . . for the students so they could follow along with her while she read . . . .

Keeping individuals, subgroups, and whole classes in mind simultaneously is necessary if teachers are to meet the needs of all learners. Teacher Wanda Freeman shows how she focuses on whole-class learning in this entry:

I must go so I can plan for a spectacular lesson tomorrow. I want/need to back up in one class because one class is having trouble setting up poetry on the paper. They do not seem to realize, no matter how many poems we read, that poetry looks a certain way . . . . We are going to do some more form poetry. I am trying to get a class set of Bronx Masquerade. *I have one copy. The kids like it but I have not gotten them to loosen up and dig deep. We will see how things go.*

Middle school teacher Michelle Harrison demonstrates how she monitors subgroups and individuals in this portion of her teaching journal:

Wed., March 24, 2004
. . . The guys did great. They love The Bully. *They seem to be responding in their journals with some success . . . . They really do use the strategies that we worked on in class . . . .*

(continues)

I have found that Alia is really coming along. She has improved in reading comprehension since we started. Now, I hope Rochelle makes some improvements also . . . . Her writing is . . . simplistic and her reading level seems to be between 5th and 6th grade.

Thurs., Apr. 15, 2004

No one is enjoying our literature. I tried to pick information on the Civil War and earth science. This is what they are studying . . . . They were not pleased; however, they are definitely transferring some strategies. Kendra said, "I should keep a journal in social studies. Maybe it will help me remember."

Mon., Apr. 19, 2004

. . . I have really noticed some growth with Colby. He's taking a turn with reading and responding in his journal . . . . He constantly calls out questions, predictions, and connections that he makes. That is so awesome because I had him in the 6th grade and I wanted him tested [for learning disabilities] because he was so low. His mother refused . . . . And now I see that this small group, interesting material, and direct instruction have helped him.

Another teacher shows how she pays careful attention to individuals in this excerpt:

The one thing that really stuck out for me in this chapter was on page 93. Cris [Tovani] says, "We can choose to cover the curriculum or we can choose to teach students to inquire. If we choose to cover the curriculum, our students will fail." . . . I just don't really feel that I have a choice. I do have students that just sit through my class like they are in a movie. I am the star and all of the students in the class are my supporting cast. I sometimes want to offer them popcorn, Junior mints, and a big Coke. One student really popped into my mind as I was reading, Charlie Evans. He reads on a first grade, fifth month level. I honestly don't know how to help this child. Also, his mother had him removed from resource. Can you imagine? . . . By using the "I wonder" questions I hope all my kids, even Charlie, will benefit. If Charlie contributes to the discussion that would be a great start. He has to wonder about something. Right?

A third-grade teacher weaves together a focus on individuals and a reflection on her own professional development in this entry:

One of my better writers . . . is completing things very quickly . . . . I don't know why this is happening . . . . My student who finishes early is grouped with higher achievers and still rushes. I also found this happening in science. Our soil kit is required to have a journal the kids write in to reflect . . . . Lyndie was the first one done but her details are not present. Maybe I can try different methods with this problem . . . . I want so badly to be the better teacher I was yesterday with more ways to improve . . . . I guess I just have to wait. I actually notice that every day brings me new experience to . . . better myself personally and professionally somehow.

Sharon Cunningham shows whole-class awareness in this piece of reflective writing:

We completed our final review of Ellen Foster *today . . . . I told the students to write down the phrase, "I wonder." They were to follow the phrase with three questions they had at the conclusion of [the book]. They looked at me like I had grown an extra eyebrow . . . . I am a little surprised by their confusion . . . . I first modeled the process. I jotted down on an overhead transparency, "I wonder what Ellen did after she moved from her foster home." . . . "I wonder what happened to Roger after Stella . . . left her foster home." I asked the students if they could find the answers in the text. They realized they were making predictions . . . . Everyone participated because they weren't threatened. They also realized that since the [book] . . . is fiction, the possibilities are infinite . . . . The students also more easily grasped the themes after digging more deeply through wondering. They saw 'the end' as really a beginning. Students were very surprised when I noted the reading strategies they were using in the process. They finally realized that they naturally used certain reading strategies; they just didn't know the names of the strategies . . . . I . . . plan on using the 'I wonder' strategy as a prewriting strategy. This . . . should help students better understand authors' techniques of slowly revealing information and stimulating interest . . . . It is so true that it is difficult to infer without first wondering. Today I could see that students were more motivated to understand the novel when they were digging deeply to ask questions . . . .*

Sometimes teachers simply need to celebrate what's going right or what they are proud of in their teaching. (Starting a journaling process by asking people to write about positives is a nonthreatening way to begin in a building, too.) Periodically, teachers should affirm themselves by writing about successes, as former teacher Kjersti Pratt did in this entry, shared with a group of teachers who participated in online, shared journaling in Horry County, South Carolina:

One thing I celebrate about my teaching is that my students see me engaged in the processes of reading and writing along with them. They know I am not a phony and that I understand the struggles they face, especially in writing. Writing is something I love to do, but that doesn't mean it's always easy for me, and I think it's important for my kids to know that. I share my process with them, but I remind them that my way is not the only way, so there might be another process that works better for them. That is another facet to my teaching that is worth celebrating—my openness to others' ideas and methods so they can figure out what works best for them. In our "test rampant" culture I think many have forgotten there is more than one right answer to the most meaningful questions and countless paths leading to those multiple answers. Today I celebrate my authenticity and receptiveness!

An art teacher celebrated her students and shared her love of her profession in this entry, also shared with others online:

My students have contributed the most to my . . . satisfaction in teaching. Their achievements and even appreciation over the years has done the most to keep me going. It has also been their desire to learn and willingness to take on new concepts and processes that [have] kept me growing as a teacher. The more they were willing to learn, the more I strived to learn so that I could pass it on to them.

So to my students I say, thank you. You have caused me to learn many new things in my desire to continue to provide you new avenues of exploration . . . . Your thirst for knowledge has kept me from stagnating. Your . . . enthusiasm has kept me much younger than my years. Your willingness to go the extra mile for me has influenced my own commitment. All of this has not only made me a better teacher, it has made me a better artist myself.

The following short entry celebrates a good day in a high school English classroom:

Another exciting class period 3rd block! I am sure that my students could be heard all the way at the front of the school building, but most all students were working, and one . . . even exclaimed . . . "I better get a good grade on this! This is the best work I've done all year!" She was so proud of her work . . . .

Sometimes teachers need to blow off steam, so to speak, and the journal is just the place to do so. One teacher in a graduate course wrote,

I wrote the word frustration *across the page. I'm with [a fellow teacher] about our time element. I feel so constrained with all our mandates for the state and district. If I take more time for this, it is taking away from that. I've been "promised" that the district plans to revamp some things this summer in reference to the [county test] and evidence folders. There is going to have to be a change in order for us to touch our students like we need in order for them to be successful readers and writers.*

A usually upbeat and confident teacher showed signs of possible future burnout in this entry:

Today is a new day, and I feel like I'm just trying to make it through . . . . I'm really disappointed in my second period class. I have about six students . . . that show absolutely NO motivation to learn about anything! I've tried all kinds of activities, but nothing seems to work. I'm so discouraged and tired of trying. Classes like this make me HATE teaching!

Most journals I have seen emphasize the positive over the negative, however. Teacher Cathy Threatt models the spirit of invention in the next excerpt, as she takes ideas she got in a presentation and discusses her own adaptations of them on the following page.

Let me tell you I took the questions Tracy [Bailey] used in her presentation and added just one. This is what I handed to my students. I added a [letter] C. I told the students to write a C anytime they could connect the text to their lives . . . . I then handed out the infamous science article Tracy used with us [in the presentation]. My students thought I had made it up to torture them. They went through and marked up the text. We discussed the text and the marks they had made. I told them that this was how you talked to a novel. I plan to do one article a week with them; I already have a neat one for next week. Now that they know how to mark a text they need to practice a lot. I also intend to photocopy a few of the chapters out of Ellen Foster *and let them mark those as we read them as a class. I have always said, "I don't know how to teach my kids to read; I don't have an elementary degree." Well, I may not have an elementary degree, but I read all the time. So showing the kids what I do when I read was something I had never even thought of . . . .*

Mary Heflin demonstrates invention in the following entry, written after reading a chapter in Cris Tovani's book *I Read It But I Don't Get It* (2000):

This chapter really gave me some food for thought. I have taught social studies as well as ELA [English language arts], and I have always known that providing . . . background for the students was very important. Learning is essentially a framework and students need to build the framework in order to incorporate new knowledge. I knew this well when I taught math, but somehow this didn't transfer when I began to teach ELA this year. When we did a novel study on The Cay, *I realized that my students needed more . . . background on World War II, the geography and climate of the setting of the story, and the prevalent attitudes of whites towards blacks . . . . I addressed these topics with maps and discussions. Before I do this novel again, I will survey the students with a KWL format to find out . . . what they want to learn. This will allow them to follow their own interests and share their knowledge with the other students. These strategies are usable and practical to me.*

The benefits of doing reflective journaling abound, and do carry over for direct impact on students. After keeping a reflective teacher's journal for a semester while in a graduate course, elementary teacher Whitney White said, "I've tried to spend more time discussing and reflecting with students. My goal is to continue having students focus on reflecting, therefore constructing more meaning from their reading and other class activities." In another entry, she said, "I've tried to have students reflect on their learning in all subject areas. My goal is to continue modeling for students how to explain and rethink about what they are learning."

Middle school teacher Gretchen Meier said, in a written reflection, that she had changed over the course of the semester: "I've become more lax in my tight control and [have] made an effort to compliment all efforts [by students]." She also noted that her goal was to "continue to encourage risks." One change she saw in her classroom was that "students are more comfortable in writing what they want, not [what] they think *I* want." She said, "I now encourage more dialogue in class," and noted that she would like to better "handle desks in groups. Very difficult for me." (Many teachers express hesitance about cooperative learning. At least this teacher knows this is something she needs to work on!) Gretchen also said, with regard to teaching the required curriculum, "I've learned that we'll get done when we're ready."

Special education teacher Cathy Green said that before her time in the Writing Project (before she kept a journal), "I had no trust in myself and preferred 'canned lessons' so I wouldn't make a mistake." In contrast, after completing the Writing Project, she said, "I now try to be more open and realize how many of my resource students are not reading/math smart, but if I integrate different intelligences, they all feel worthwhile."

Former teacher Ruby Hart said she found herself talking less and letting students explore more for answers. She also set a personal goal to minimize class disruptions during cooperative grouping. (This is a concern that many teachers have noted and that sometimes keeps them from using cooperative learning strategies.) Ruby also cited another new instructional strategy: "letting students find their own interesting vocabulary in a reading selection instead of relying on chosen textbook vocabulary." She also specified one thing she did differently in her classes: "We share more about how to think things through." Her students, she reported, were "learning more concept[s], less facts."

High school teacher Sharon Cunningham wrote regarding guided reading, an instructional strategy,

I realized I had been mixing a little too much guided with my shared [reading] . . . . I had been guiding the readers through the text too much instead of guiding their reading by encouraging strategies. Several years ago I was truly horrible with literal interpretation questions. Last year I trimmed those questions quite a bit and focused more on strategies. Improvement was very obvious. Students were much more comfortable and confident with the reading strategies.

High school teacher Diane Starnes worked through the entire ARRIVE cycle in her teaching journal one semester as she enacted an inquiry project for a graduate course. She assessed the need for her students to have greater fluency and comprehension in reading. She decided to implement 25 minutes of daily independent reading with her sophomores so they would be better prepared to take the state's graduation test (called the Exit Exam) in the spring. She looked at their previous standardized test scores (from eighth grade) in addition to giving them a teacher-made questionnaire asking them about their perceptions of reading. She also administered a STAR diagnostic test and conducted a miscue analysis to determine fluency. She used the Brigance test to determine current level of comprehension. Then, a couple of months after using the independent reading strategy, she retested them, verifying her success and their academic achievement.

At the beginning of her inquiry, only 19 percent of her students said reading was very important in their lives; 31 percent thought it was not very important, and the others thought it was "somewhat important." Twenty-six percent of the students disliked reading, whereas 50 percent thought it was just "okay." The others said they liked it. Fifty-six percent of her students said they did not see themselves as readers. Eleven percent believed that reading was only the ability to say the words on the page (decoding).

As measured by the Peabody Individual Achievement Test—Revised, Diane's students, on average, gained 2.2 reading levels in comprehension in only two months. The largest gain was one student whose comprehension went from grade level 4.4 to 9.3. Of the eight students she tracked, *every single one showed statistically significant growth in reading comprehension as a result of her teaching.*

Diane saw her teaching change and her confidence grow:

My teaching has been completely revolutionized . . . as have my students! My kids who hated to read now love it! I have two girls reading It Happened to Nancy *together. One of the girls has always hated to read. She made the comment yesterday that she can't wait for lunch to be over so she can come in and find out what happens next in the book! The other student thanked me . . . for giving them time to read in class . . . . Wow!*

About the same two girls, Diane wrote:

Tawny is the super-reluctant reader who on the first day of school told me, "You know I ain't going to read no book." . . . She's also the one . . . doing a shared reading . . . with another student . . . and last week said she couldn't wait for lunch to be over to find out what happened next. Friday Tawny had to leave school early, so she asked if she could take a copy of the book home so she would not be behind when she came back . . . . Well, [she] came in this morning and told me not to be mad at her . . . . She read the entire book this weekend! She was only supposed to read to page 60 but finished all 218 pages! She said she couldn't put it down, and her mother was wondering what was wrong with her. She would fall asleep at night reading and it would fall out of her hands; her mother would . . . mark which page she was on . . . . I think I just may have her hooked now!

Diane also demonstrates how her own journaling influenced the direction her classes took:

My students are getting better at questioning the authors and text they are reading. They initially just assumed everything was perfect because it was in print, but as they are becoming more involved in their texts, they are beginning to critique the work more . . . . At times we wonder why we bother, then we have that one student that makes us realize exactly why we're doing it. I have to say there are definitely days when I want to strangle my students, but then I get responses in their journals like, "I'm so happy we're keeping a journal every day in here . . . it really helps me get out my thoughts and feel better. After I've finished this journal, I'm going to keep it as a diary of this year." While I know not all of my students love writing in their journals . . . , I do believe most of them do. I think what matters most to them is that I respond to each one of their entries every day. If something comes up to where I don't have time to respond, some of them won't write me the next day until I write them back first. While it is a good bit of work to read and respond . . . daily, I believe that the end results are well worth the extra effort.

High school English teacher Jan Vescovi assessed her students' needs to enjoy reading more and to improve their comprehension. She looked at the previous year's standardized test scores and gave a pretest of her own design in the assess stage of ARRIVE. She selected the strategies of teacher read-alouds, SSR, book pass, book talks, think-alouds, marking the text, a graphic organizer for vocabulary, and a reading log/journal. (These strategies came from talking with colleagues and from reading professional books by Janet Allen and Cris Tovani.) Jan documented incremental improvement in her teaching journal throughout the year and has made a teaching journal part of her practice.

Frank Clark, a teacher who has taught high school juniors and seniors for more than 20 years, thinks that the reflective journal is an ideal tool for students; he also writes in a journal himself. He said, "Journaling helps me better express what I am feeling . . . . [It] can be very creative, and all of us need that feeling of newness. Any time you stop to reflect and organize, you are going to be more productive in whatever you do." He sees a possible connection to professional development for teachers: "Most staff development has merit, but if more was about journaling and its benefits, teachers would carry away from the session an eagerness to write and contemplate more."

Australian educator Julie Boyd compared her learning to the learning of students in her journal:

I know that for me the process is the same regardless of whether I'm learning to dive, to program a microwave, or speak in public—I have to actually be given enough information to feel confident . . . and then think and talk about all the things I did and need to do . . . . Maybe one of the things I'll try with the kids is talking with them about what I've learned and then give them more time to think things through first before I expect them to put pen to paper. Figuring out how to do that and keep on task will be interesting (Dalton & Boyd, 1992, p. 103).

David Gorman, in an article in the *Journal of Adolescent and Adult Literacy*, wrote eloquently about the power of journaling, so I will close this chapter with his words:

Many teachers, including me, fail to improve . . . because we refuse to break from patterns that bind us. Last year, I didn't keep a teacher journal. Instead, I loosely worked with ideas in my head. If a particular technique worked well for one class, I would use it for the next class. Unfortunately, this method allowed little in the way of concrete assessment examples that could be evaluated over time. Also, without a journal, I wasn't as accountable to myself. It was extremely easy to think of a weakness in teaching strategy and then do nothing about it . . . . With a journal, the classroom problems are recorded on paper. The likelihood of change in instructional decision making is greater because the teacher is more accountable . . . (1998).

Later in the piece, he concluded:

Just writing ideas on the page isn't enough. Teachers must act on their written impulses. Once we, as teachers, act, we need to record whether success occurred or not. The process must continue . . . until we have found a nearly perfect way to present a given body of work in our particular teaching style. Good journal writing can always help toward that aim. I will continue to use my journal for years to come as a tool for literacy development and learning.

How Can Supervisors and
Staff Developers Use **Journaling?**

Using reflective journaling costs very little but brings in huge rewards, not only for teachers, but also for those who supervise them and others who facilitate professional development.

I arise in the morning torn between a desire to improve (or save) the world and a desire to enjoy (or savor) the world. This makes it hard to plan the day.
— E. B. White

Suggested Timelines and Journal Prompts

In my first leadership role outside of the classroom, I was charged with assisting 27 teachers in grades K–12 as they implemented new curriculum standards. They were also incorporating the use of new computers and software. Even though I had plenty of experience as a high school teacher, I found myself struggling with the one group of high school teachers with whom I met regularly.

Two of the teachers were so dependent on lecture and whole-group instruction that I thought I would never be able to get them to try innovative methods, much less embrace technology. However, after one memorable staff development meeting, I saw a glimmer of hope, as evidenced in my journal entry written January 11, 1996.

What I learned: that even reluctant-to-change teachers get excited about technology; that technology is a hook that will get the [instructional coaches] into the classrooms doing active, meaningful work; and that sometimes a small step is a large one. When Shelly and Joan got excited about learning some of the features of Word, I got excited, too. They're starting on a journey that will enhance all they do as teachers.

In the fall preceding that session, I didn't sound as optimistic:

I'm always happy to be in my pilot teachers' classrooms, even though I feel as if I need to spend about a whole week with each person! An hour or two every couple of weeks is simply not enough time to even begin to understand the context in which each teacher is working.

I've been rereading the **SC English Language Arts Framework** *(for about the 100th time) and thinking about the classrooms I've visited so far. One thing I haven't seen consistently is a literacy-rich environment. I know that school budgets are increasingly tight, but . . . a language arts classroom* must *be full of LANGUAGE. Many teachers spend their own money to fill their rooms with books . . . I know I always did—but why do we* have *to? Perhaps one result of this project will be that we recommend what all English classrooms need to best serve children . . . classroom libraries that include classics and young adult literature. Next, more computers. Each room needs to be a mini-lab . . . .*

. . . Next topic: daily reading and writing. I've seen a few instances of students reading independently, but in short bursts . . . . I've seen a couple of teachers read aloud to students, but only excerpts. How do we make sure we provide more time devoted to reading?

As for writing, I've caught the tail-end of some journal-writing times. I've seen "small" writing tasks, like friendly letters and descriptive paragraphs. But I haven't seen students engaged in multi-draft, long-term writing . . . . And I haven't seen teachers writing. Modeling the habits of mind required . . . is emphasized in the Framework. Also, it just makes sense. I can't ask students to do what I'm unwilling to do.

When will my teachers examine the BIG PICTURE?

Writing in my reflective journal helped me set the pace of the project, plan meetings, vent my frustrations, and celebrate successes, no matter how small. I often drafted various conversations in my journal that I would then have with small groups or individual teachers; this helped me be proactive instead of reactive and helped me be prepared for any contingency.

The following interview, conducted with Janet Files, staff developer and teacher of undergraduate and graduate education courses, highlights how she came to use journaling and the benefits she perceives.

1. *Can you discuss how you came to include journaling in your practice (both in working with preservice teachers and with the National Writing Project)?*

    Janet: I believe that we don't just learn from experience but by reflecting on that experience. The act of writing about a complex process[,] such as creating written compositions[,] helps my students reflect . . . for current insights and future action. Since most of my students have never experienced a supportive, process-oriented approach to writing, I immerse them in an authentic writing process. Through this immersion, they begin to see themselves as writers and to value the process. This helps them create a new vision for what writing instruction might look and feel like. However, the lived-through process is not enough for teachers . . . . Teachers must also be able to recreate this writing process for their own students. By writing reflectively each day about what they learned about themselves as writers and what they value for their own learning, we are able to unpack the very organic, recursive writing process, name what matters and begin to create a theory in action.

    Likewise, I use journaling to reflect on my own process in order to constantly pay attention to what responses my students have to my intentional teaching and to gain insights into how to adjust my teaching and help lift their learning.

2. *How do you use reflective journals — either the traditional written type, responses to reading, or electronic/online journals — in your South Carolina Reading Initiative work?*

Janet: In the South Carolina Reading Initiative, we work with coaches for four years. This is a remarkable opportunity to develop a community of thinking and learning together. Our coaches come to state[wide] study three days a month to immerse themselves in best practice and to read and discuss research that supports this practice. They return to their home schools to lead study groups of teachers and share this same process with the teachers, as well as supporting them in classroom coaching. I act as both their teacher in state[wide] study and as a regional coach who visits five of the coaches on site once a month in their home schools. I use many forms of reflective journals to help the coaches think through their learning as well as to communicate with me so I can see what new connections they are making . . . . We write reflections on our professional readings, using varied forms of response to push our thinking and hold our thoughts still so we can engage in professional literature discussion . . . . We have used a double entry journal, sketch to stretch [Harste, Short, & Burke, 1989], as well as a conversation grid that involves listing "likes, dislikes, patterns and wonders." We also occasionally have a "write around" where we talk on paper about our reading or issues in our learning and practice. This strategy is a kind of "living journal" that helps learners pay attention to formulating their own thoughts as they write them on paper as well as creating a safe space to "listen" in on others' thinking. For "write around," I pose a question or talking point issue and ask small groups to respond on paper, passing every two or three minutes, when I say "pass" and responding to the written conversation in the round. After a reasonable amount of time, we stop the pass and check off the repeated lines of thinking by looking for patterns. Then these issues are brought forward to the whole group for large group discussion. The written conversation in the round is collected . . . and helps me have a record of what everyone is thinking so I can reflect on what they are learning and build my teaching on this.

I also use a continuous "journal" of sorts in class. Since the teachers are with me full days of six hours each in our state[wide] study, there is much new information that the coaches try to think through. In order to help them hold onto their thinking I have created what I call "pause and ponder" papers. The coaches "pause" at one or two intervals during the day to reflect on paper on some question or issue. Often we use this to gather our individual thoughts around an issue before a small or large group discussion. Writing has the power to call forth more carefully formed thoughts than just talking. Writing has the added feature of creating a record over time of one's thinking so that change over time is evident. I use [carbonless] . . . paper in duplicate for this reflective writing so that the coach can keep a copy . . . . I collect these at the end of the day and return them to the coach, sometimes with comments and answers to their questions so that they can keep a copy and I have a copy for my records. I use "pause and ponder" reflections in my summer writing project institute for the same purposes.

3. *What evidence have you seen of reflective journals being used by teachers . . . increas[ing] . . . student achievement? An example would be a teacher who preplans lessons in a journal and then goes back to write about the student results after teaching the lesson.*

Janet: We have created some forms of reflective journaling to help coaches become more reflective, intentional learners and teachers. As coaches, they are supporting the change process for approximately 20 teachers through study groups and classroom coaching. The coaches have used a responsive teaching cycle process throughout their SCRI experience. One form we have tried for this has three parts—observations, reflections and new plans. The coaches keep notes on what they observe in the classrooms they work in, or on their study groups. They then make reflective notes on what insights they gain from these observations. Finally they create intentional plans based on their original goals for learning, the observed results of their intentional teaching, and the changes they will make or new actions they will try in order to build on their insights gained. We share these responsive teaching cycle notes in small groups to help each other become more insightful about their teaching.

This responsive teaching has enormous results. Prior to this kind of reflection, the coaches noted that often, they and the teachers would not pay attention to learner responses as much as they do now. The emphasis was more on covering and teaching a curriculum than on teaching the learner—and adjusting the curriculum to meet the needs of the learner. These reflective observation journals help the teachers continuously assess whether learning has occurred and what to do to ensure learning.

Once a month the coaches write "one pagers" in response to their coaching. They read over their reflections for the month and think on paper to me about what insights they are gaining, what new questions they have and help me know what they have been working through. These one pagers help me teach the coaches in a much more responsive way, as I see once again how the teaching at the state study has played out in their actual teaching lives at their home schools.

4. *Is there anything else you want to say to convince other educators to use reflective writing/journaling activities in professional development?*

Janet: I can't imagine supporting teachers' learning without the ongoing conversation that reflective journaling provides. The various ways to journal about their own practice allow teachers to have an ongoing conversation with themselves that helps them gain more confidence and voice in their teaching. When the journals are shared with the professional development leader, they provide invaluable insights into individual learners and allow for the instruction to be an ongoing lively conversation that is responsive and inquiry-based.

Larry Ainsworth, a consultant for the Center for Performance Assessment and an education writer, also advocates journaling (personal communication, 2005):

Reflective journaling is a practice I've used for nearly ten years to help process the volume of information that inundates my mind on a continual basis. It has become such a valuable part of my daily regimen that I can't imagine either starting or ending my day without it. Journaling helps me determine my short- and long-term priorities, make clear-thinking decisions, and "listen to the still small voice" of intuition within. I use this practice in all aspects of my life, including my educational career. As a sixth grade teacher, I taught my 34 students how to journal and provided them with a "safe" environment in which to practice each morning before beginning academic study. Many told me it was the best part of their day. I cannot recommend this practice too highly. Journaling enables me to stay aligned to my life's purpose.

Journaling at Your School Site

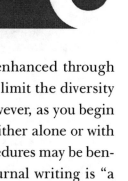

"Journal writing is as varied as those who engage in it," wrote David Boud (2001, p. 9), in an article about journaling in New Directions for Adult and Continuing Education.

Learning is not compulsory . . . neither is survival.

—J. Edwards Deming

Diversity is promoted and creativity is enhanced through journaling; I, for one, would not seek to limit the diversity by recommending specific protocols. However, as you begin a journaling process at your school site, either alone or with like-minded others, some consistent procedures may be beneficial. As Boud noted in his article, journal writing is "a vehicle for learning" (2001, p. 9). To maximize learning for participants, initial ground rules and structure may be helpful. I will offer suggestions throughout this chapter for your consideration.

First, to set the tone for learning, it must be made clear to the participants whether there will ever be an audience other than one's self for the journals. If you are engaging in reflective journaling independently, this is obviously a decision you and you alone will make; but if journaling in its various forms will be undertaken in meetings and inservices, then the purpose and audience must be made clear each time. If verbal journaling prompts are used, the audience is clear, because the audience is present to hear the conversation. If written, art, and electronic forms of journaling are used, the audience may change from time to time, and thus must be stated every time.

Laura Aten undertook journal writing within a group of 16 experienced middle school teachers over a period of ten weeks and studied the process as a basis for her dissertation. The teachers responded to two prompts per week. Aten found that keeping a journal "fostered many levels of reflection" and that the participants "found professional value in keeping a journal" (2003, p. vi). School staffs or small groups within school staffs may find that a structured process, such as the one Aten used, is helpful as the process is initiated.

Once teachers are in the habit of writing, journal prompts may become unnecessary because they will feel restrictive. For a group just starting out, though, prompts can provide a welcome structure. The following are some prompts I have used successfully over the years with different groups (graduate students, teachers involved in instructional coaching, faculty members participating in inservice sessions, and participants in one-time workshops). Consider using them or revising them as you see fit.

1. Describe the ideal classroom. What is the teacher doing? What are the students doing? What resources are on hand? What does one see and hear?

2. When you are teaching at your best, to what or whom could you compare yourself? What are you like? What is your classroom like?

3. Write about a lesson that went well. What can you learn from this episode?

4. Write about a memorable student. Perhaps it's one who defied your expectations or one whom you felt was unreachable. Perhaps it's one who taught you more than you feel you taught him or her.

5. Write about a lesson or unit you know you will teach again. How will you change it to make it better?

Reflective journaling can be helpful as teachers deal with big changes, such as a change of leadership in the school, a new mandated curriculum, or an influx of very different students. I had one such experience during the 1995–1996 school year, as I worked with 27 K–12 teachers to make new state curriculum standards come to life in their classrooms. Each teacher received five new classroom computers (among other perks), and in return, agreed to attend weekly meetings, develop one publishable performance assessment, be observed repeatedly, and keep a reflective journal. The prompts I used that year were as follows. You will see how you can adapt them for your own use if you are working with new standards, assessments, and/or technology.

1. How do you teach to the standards in your classroom?

2. Describe lessons, strategies, resources, or plans you'd like to enact and relate them to specific standards.

3. How do you apply multiple-intelligences research in your classroom? Which of the intelligences do you feel you incorporate well? Which are hard for you to incorporate?

4. Are there students you feel have mastered certain standards? Describe them and their work.

5. Are there students you feel will have trouble meeting certain standards? Describe them and their work. Propose solutions.

6. What has been a successful lesson, project, unit, or activity in your classroom? Describe it and tell why you feel it was successful.

7. What are you considering for the model performance assessment you will write soon? Start drafting.

8. How are you expanding your use of technology personally and with your students?

9. Look at the "chunk" of learning you and your students are involved in right now. How will you assess their learning at the end of this "chunk"? How have you identified and communicated the expected learning?

10. How do we assess vocabulary in a more authentic, performance-oriented manner?

11. How do we facilitate students having meaningful conferences about the content of their writing before they peer-edit?

12. How do we manage to give all students adequate, meaningful time on computers without turning the room into total chaos?

If you have the good fortune to be the person facilitating a journaling process, you may want to share your first response with the group, either by providing a copy of it or simply by talking about it, saying, "I wrote about . . . ." Just an informal sharing can open up productive conversations and ease the trepidation others may be feeling.

Another good way to begin is to base the journal writing on a common text, such as a professional book. One of the best out there is the book *Mind Matters: Teaching for Thinking* (Kirby & Kuykendall, 1991). Another excellent choice is *The Teacher's Daybook 2004-2005: Time to Teach, Time to Learn, Time to Live* (2004), by Jim Burke, an English teacher and prolific writer of professional materials. This combination planner, organizer, and reflective journal is a tool that could be employed many times throughout the school year.

Using journaling in combination with a data monitoring process as part of the ARRIVE teaching cycle can be quite beneficial for teachers. Writing, even in five-minute spurts, can be undertaken at any step in the process and can lead to new insights. What will support a particular teacher and get her or him to try new strategies or view another problem within the cycle?

Certainly the culture of the school and the larger organization of which the school is a part is also critical. How can you be reflective in a building where experimentation is frowned upon or where the administrators dictate every move or change direction like people change their socks? (I have worked in a place like this, and try as I might, I could not get any deep reflection going because the culture suppressed it.) If experimentation and innovation are devalued, the reflective teaching cycle will fail and journaling will not work. It is best to have teachers undertaking personalized reflection instead. If you are a teacher-leader in such a school, start using reflective methods yourself first, and then think about how you can spread the word.

Reflective teaching can be as private as a teacher wants. Except for the research part of the ARRIVE cycle, maybe, no one even needs to know what you are doing, if you are in a school or organizational culture that would look askance at your ideas. If you're an introvert, your research can consist of professional reading, or attending conference sessions or other inservices, and then letting your reflection occur in your private journal. You need only look back through it on perhaps a monthly basis, to glean new insights and to better understand your own growth. Then again, maybe you feel comfortable enough to share your ideas with one trusted colleague. That's enough to begin with.

The reflective teaching process mirrors the writing process—so what better than to marry the two with a journal? A written artifact—how appropriate! Get started!

Appendix A: Example of the *Assess Stage* in the ARRIVE Reflective Teaching Cycle

1. alliteration
2. allusion
3. exaggeration
4. figurative language
5. free verse
6. idiom
7. imagery
8. lyric poetry
9. metaphor
10. mood
11. narrative poem
12. onomatopoeia
13. personification
14. repetition
15. rhyme
16. rhyme scheme
17. simile
18. stanza symbol tone and voice
19. symbol
20. tone and voice

Listed above are poetry elements. Authors use these elements to help their poetry come alive, to help you see it, feel it, smell it, taste it, and hear it. Not all elements are used in every poem, but every poem will have some elements in it. Test your knowledge of the terms. See which ones you can identify in the following "Words" poem. (Not all of the listed elements are used in this poem.)

What do you see:

1. in line 2? _____
2. in lines 6 and 7? _____
3. in lines 1, 11, 21, and 33? _____
4. in lines 13, 14, and 15? _____
5. in line 17? _____
6. in lines 18 and 19? _____
7. in line 23? _____
8. in line 27? _____

   9. in lines 35, 36, 37, and 38? _____

  10. in lines 1–10, 11–20,
       21–32, and 33–43?   _____

  11. in lines 28 and 29?   _____

Answer the following questions about the "Words" poem:

  1. The "Words" poem is a _____ poem and not a
    _____ poem because _____ .

  2. The rhyme scheme of the third stanza is _____ .

  3. State your opinion. For what symbol do you think *words* stands for
    this author?

  4. What mood does this poem evoke in you? What mood do you think
    the author feels?

  5. Identify a line or two that uses examples of imagery.

Words

Words! I love them!
Wild, wiggly, wobbly words
Words that tell a story
Words that tell a lie
5   *Words that reach*
All the way up to the sky
I love the ones that stretch a mile
And even the ones that
Make me cry
10   *Or want to sleep for a very long while.*

Words! I love them!
Wet, wishy, washy words

Jonah and the whale words
Wonderland words of mad hatters
15   *And rabbits that talk.*
I love words that
Sound like music to my ears
And words that are little
Drops of gold spreading priceless
20   *Bits of wisdom throughout the year.*

Words! I love them!
Weird, bewitching, wacky words
Words that drive me up the wall
Words so long they always fall
25   *Wrecklessly over my teeth and tongue*
Like alphabet soup.
I love words that put us all in groups
That fear the dark of midnight dreary
Or love the mid day so bright and cheery
30   *With air so fresh, or sun so hot,*
Or buds that smell like my granddad's yard
When I played there in my winsome youth.

Words! I love them!
Whimsical, wired, warm words
35   *Words that whiz and crash*
And bang and buzz
And screech and eek
And clank and thud
I love words, all kinds of words
40   *But I think my favorite words*
Of all the words
Are three little words that mean a lot:
43   *A plethora of.*

Wanda Smith Freeman (March 1, 2004)

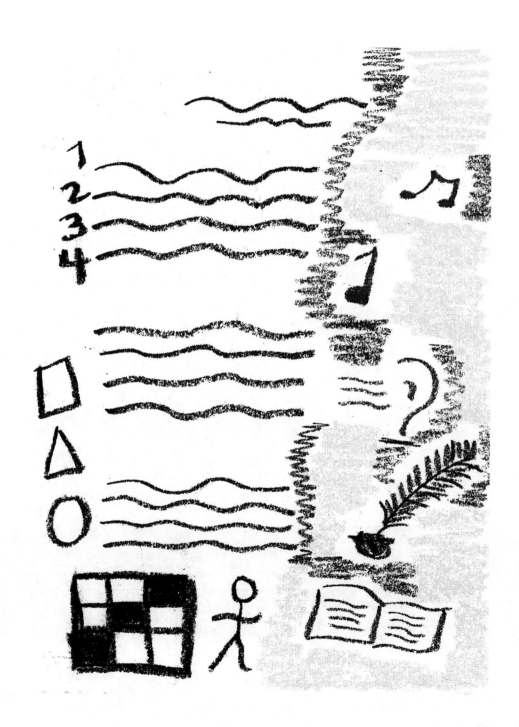

Appendix C: Symbolic Representation of a Metaphor for Teaching II

When I teach well, I am a hummingbird: graceful, busy, going where I need to when I'm supposed to. Alighting on children, doing my job, and moving on quickly.

*Artwork courtesy of Cathy Green, elementary school special education teacher.

Appendix D: Summary of the ARRIVE Cycle

A = ASSESS

- Determine the need or problem.
- Take a baseline measurement.
- Set a student achievement goal.

R = RESEARCH

- Immerse yourself in study of the need or problem.

R = REFLECT

- Select possible solutions after deliberation.

I = INNOVATE

- Employ the solutions in the classroom.

V = VERIFY

- Measure student achievement based on the goal you set.

E = EVALUATE

- Determine next steps.

Appendix E: Reflective Journal Prompts Used Successfully with Groups of Teachers

The following journal topics were used in a project I led for Horry County Schools during the 1995–1996 school year. I worked with 27 teachers of grades K–12 to make new state curriculum standards come to life in their classrooms. Each teacher received five new classroom computers (among other perks); in return, each teacher agreed to attend weekly meetings, develop one publishable performance assessment, be observed repeatedly, and keep a reflective journal.

- How do you teach to the standards in your classroom?

- Describe lessons, strategies, resources, or plans you'd like to enact and relate them to specific standards.

- How do you apply multiple-intelligences research in your classroom? Which of the intelligences do you feel you incorporate well? Which are hard for you to incorporate?

- Are there students you feel have mastered certain standards? Describe them and their work.

- Are there students you feel will have trouble meeting certain standards? Describe them and their work. Propose solutions.

- What has been a successful lesson, project, unit, or activity in your classroom? Describe it and tell why you feel it was successful.

- What are you considering for the model performance assessment you will write soon? Start drafting.

- How are you expanding your use of technology personally and with your students?

- Look at the "chunk" of learning you and your students are involved in right now. How will you assess their learning at the end of this "chunk"? How have you identified and communicated the expected learning?

- How do we assess vocabulary in a more authentic, performance-oriented manner?

- How do we facilitate students' having meaningful conferences about the content of their writing before they peer-edit?

- How do we manage to give all students adequate, meaningful time on computers without turning the room into total chaos?

References

Ainsworth, L. (2003). *Power standards: Identifying the standards that matter the most.* Englewood, CO: Advanced Learning Press.

Allen, J. (2004, July 29). Keynote address at meeting of the Literacy Leadership Institute, Columbia, SC.

Aten, L. (2003). *Using guided journals to foster reflection and professional judgment in teachers.* Unpublished doctoral dissertation, University of Texas at San Antonio.

Boud, D. (2001). Using journal writing to enhance reflective practice. *New Directions for Adult and Continuing Education, 90,* 9–17.

Brainydictionary.com. (n.d.). Retrieved July 29, 2004 from http://www.brainy-dictionary.com/words/jo/journal181743.html

Brewster, C., & Railsback, J. (2001). *Supporting new teachers: How administrators, teachers, and policymakers can help teachers succeed.* Portland, OR: Northwest Regional Educational Laboratory.

Brookfield, S. (1995). *Becoming a critically reflective teacher.* San Francisco: Jossey-Bass.

Brooks, J. G. (2004, September). To see beyond the lesson. *Educational Leadership, 62*(1), 8–13.

Burke, C., & Short, K. (1991). *Creating curriculum: Teachers and students as a community of learners.* Portsmouth, NH: Heinemann.

Burke, J. (2004). *The teacher's daybook 2004-2005: Time to teach, time to learn, time to live.* Portsmouth, NH: Boynton/Cook.

Campbell, A. (1993). *Your corner of the universe.* Holbrook, MA: Bob Adams, Inc.

Dalton, J., & Boyd, J. (1992). *I teach: A guide to inspiring classroom leadership.* Portsmouth, NH: Heinemann.

Dewey, J. (1958). How we think. In W. B. Kolesnick, *Mental discipline in modern education.* Madison: University of Wisconsin Press.

Dewey, J. (1916). Democracy and education. Retrieved August 16, 2004 from http://www.ilt.columbia.edu/academic/texts/dewey

Eisner, E. (2004). Artistry in teaching. Retrieved March 29, 2005 from http://www.culturalcommons.org/eisner.htm

Farrell, T. (2004). *Reflective practice in action: 80 reflection breaks for busy teachers.* Thousand Oaks: CA: Corwin Press.

Freeman, D. (1996). Redefining the relationship between research and what teachers know. In K. M. Bailey & D. Nunan (Eds.), *Voices from the language classroom: Qualitative research in second language education* (pp. 88–115). Cambridge: Cambridge University Press.

Fullan, M., with Stiegelbauer, S. (1991). *The new meaning of educational change.* New York: Teachers College Press.

Gorman, D. (1998). Self-tuning teachers: Using reflective journals in writing classes. *Journal of Adolescent & Adult Literacy, 41*(6), 434–443.

Greenberg, J. S. (1999). *Comprehensive stress management* (6th ed.). Boston: McGraw-Hill. Quoted in *Understanding and preventing teacher burnout.* ERIC Digest. ARC Professional Services Group, ED Contract No. RI89002001. (ERIC Document Reproduction Service No. ED477726).

Harste, J., Short, K., & Burke, C. (1989). *Creating classrooms for authors.* Portsmouth, NH: Heinemann.

Haycock, K. (1999). Good teaching matters a lot. Retrieved August 16, 2004, from http://www.nsdc.org/library/publications/results/res3-99haycock.cfm

Jensen, E. (1998). *Teaching with the brain in mind.* Alexandria, VA: Association for Supervision and Curriculum Development.

Kirby, D., & Kuykendall, C. (1991). *Mind matters: Teaching for thinking.* Portsmouth, NH: Boynton/Cook.

Knowles, M. S. (1980). *The modern practice of adult education: From andragogy to pedagogy.* Englewood Cliffs, NJ: Cambridge Adult Education.

Lieberman, A. (2000, March). *Teachers transforming teaching: Stories, strategies, and structures.* Session presented at the Teaching for Thinking Conference, Orlando, FL.

Marzano, R. J., Pickering, D. J., & Pollock, J. E. (2004). *Classroom instruction that works.* Englewood, CO: Advanced Learning Press.

Merriam-Webster Dictionary (online). (2001). Retrieved August 16, 2004 from http://rl.channel.aol.com/references

National Board for Professional Teaching Standards. (n.d.a). Retrieved March 29, 2005 from http://www.nbpts.org/about/coreprops.cfm#prop4

National Board for Professional Teaching Standards. (n.d.b). Retrieved March 29, 2005 from (http://www.nbpts.org/candidates/guide/04port/ 04_ ayaela_instructions/04_aya_ela_intro.pdf)

National Commission on Teaching and America's Future. (1996). What matters most: Teaching for America's future. Retrieved March 30, 2005 from http://www.nctaf.org/documents/nctaf/WhatMattersMost.pdf

National Staff Development Council [NSDC]. (2004). *Standards for staff development.* Retrieved November 15, 2004 from http://www.nsdc.org/standards/qualityteaching.cfm

References

Nieto, S., Gordon, S., & Yearwood, J. (2002). Teachers' experiences in a critical inquiry group: A conversation in three voices. *Teaching Education, 13*(3), 341–355. Retrieved March 30, 2005 from http://taylorandfrancis.metapress.com/app/home/contribution.asp?wasp=a656bd0a7af04f8 9b63c79d40085b28d&referrer=parent&backto=issue,7,9;journal,8,16;linkingpublicationresults,1:105360,1

Ray, K. W. (n.d.) Retrieved March 25, 2005 from http://www.readinglady.com/mosaic/tools/KatieWoodRayworshopnotesbyLori.pdf

Reeves, D. (2004). *Making standards work: How to implement standards-based assessment in the classroom, school, and district.* Englewood, CO: Advanced Learning Press.

Reeves, D. (2002.) *The daily disciplines of leadership: How to improve student achievement, staff motivation, and personal organization.* San Francisco: Jossey-Bass.

Richardson, J. (1999). Learning benefits everyone. *Journal of Staff Development.* Retrieved March 30, 2005 from http://www.nsdc.org/library/publications/jsd/richardson211.pdf

Rothstein, E., & Lauber, G. (2000). *Writing as learning: A content-based approach.* Glenview, IL: Pearson Skylight.

Ruhland, S. (n.d.). *Factors influencing the turnover and retention of Minnesota's secondary career and technical education teachers.* Unpublished doctoral dissertation, St. Paul, Minnesota, University of Minnesota.

Schön, D. (1983). *The reflective practitioner: How professionals think in action.* New York: Basic Books.

Senge, P. 1994. *The fifth discipline: The art and practice of the learning organization.* New York: Doubleday.

Smyth, J., et al. (1999). Effects of writing about stressful experiences on symptom reduction in patients with asthma or rheumatoid arthritis. *Journal of the American Medical Association, 281,* 1304–1309.

Sparks, D. (2004.) A call to creativity. *Journal of Staff Development, 25*(1); retrieved March 29, 2005 from www.nsdc.org

Starlings, C., McLean, D., & Moran, P. (2002). *Teacher attrition and special education in Alaska.* [Research report; n.p.: n.p.]

Tovani, C. (2000). *I read it, but I don't get it.* Portland, ME: Stenhouse.

Whited, Amy. (2005). *The reflection journal.* Englewood, CO: Advanced Learning Press.

WholeHealthMD. (2000). Retrieved August 16, 2004, from http://www.wholehealthmd.com/refshelf/ substances_view/1,1525,745,00.html

Index

Index

vocabulary, 38, 39–40, 59–60
  assessing, 76, 89

W

White, Whitney, 59
working conditions and hours, 4
write arounds, 68
writing, 22, 32, 40, 77. *See also*
  journaling; poetry
  improving, 52
  modeling, 56, 66
  persuasive, 13
  process, 67, 76, 77, 90
  for reflection, 67, 69
writing therapy, 2
written journals, 35, 37–40, 74
  entry types, 49–50

Center for Performance Assessment

Do you believe all students can succeed?

Can educators make a difference and produce results?

So much to do and so little time!

Since 1992, school districts and educational organizations seeking to improve student achievement have consulted with the Center for Performance Assessment. Educational leaders on five continents have collaboratively created customized solutions based on research and results. If you would like to know more about the services of the Center for Performance Assessment, to learn about success stories for every type of educational setting, to find out about the latest research, or to arrange a presentation by a Center consultant, please visit the Web site at www.MakingStandardsWork.com or contact:

CENTER FOR
PERFORMANCE
ASSESSMENT

Success for every student.

317 Inverness Way South, Suite 150 ▪ Englewood, CO 80112

(800) 844-6599 or (303) 504-9312 ▪ Fax (303) 504-9417